The South Atlantic Coast
and Piedmont

The *Stories from Where We Live* Series

Each volume in the *Stories from Where We Live* series celebrates a North American ecoregion through its own distinctive literature. For thousands of years, people have told stories to convey their community's cultural and natural history. *Stories from Where We Live* reinvigorates that tradition in hopes of helping young people better understand the place where they live. The anthologies feature poems, stories, and essays from historical and contemporary authors, as well as from the oral traditions of each region's indigenous peoples. Together they document the geographic richness of the continent and reflect the myriad ways that people interact with and respond to the natural world. We hope that these stories kindle readers' imaginations and inspire them to explore, observe, ponder, and protect the place they call home.

Please visit www.milkweed.org for a teaching guide to this book and more information on the *Stories from Where We Live* series.

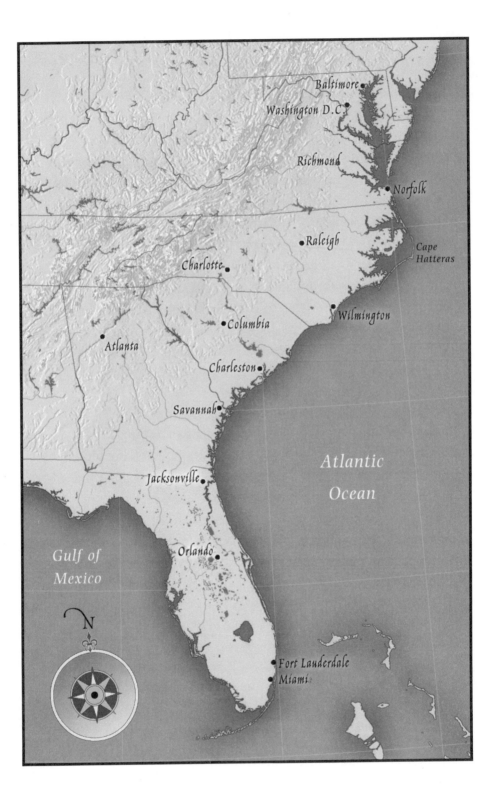

The South Atlantic Coast and Piedmont

Stories from Where We Live

EDITED BY SARA ST. ANTOINE

Maps by Paul Mirocha
Illustrations by Trudy Nicholson

MILKWEED EDITIONS

Published 2006 by Milkweed Editions
Printed in Canada
Illustrations by Trudy Nicholson
Maps by Paul Mirocha
Interior design by Wendy Holdman
The text of this book is set in Legacy.
06   07   08   09   10   5   4   3   2   1
First Paperback Edition

Milkweed Editions, a nonprofit publisher, gratefully acknowledges sustaining support from
Emilie and Henry Buchwald; Bush Foundation; Patrick and Aimee Butler Family Foundation;
Cargill Value Investment; Timothy and Tara Clark Family Charitable Fund; Dougherty
Family Foundation; Ecolab Foundation; General Mills Foundation; John and Joanne
Gordon; Greystone Foundation; Institute for Scholarship in the Liberal Arts, College of Arts
and Sciences, University of Notre Dame; Constance B. Kunin; Marshall BankFirst; Marshall
Field's Gives; May Department Stores Company Foundation; McKnight Foundation; a grant
from the Minnesota State Arts Board, through an appropriation by the Minnesota State
Legislature, a grant from the National Endowment for the Arts, and private funders; an award
from the National Endowment for the Arts, which believes that a great nation deserves great
art; Navarre Corporation; Debbie Reynolds; St. Paul Travelers Foundation; Ellen and Sheldon
Sturgis; Target Foundation; Gertrude Sexton Thompson Charitable Trust (George R. A.
Johnson, Trustee); James R. Thorpe Foundation; Toro Foundation; Serene and Christopher
Warren; W. M. Foundation; and Xcel Energy Foundation.

Library of Congress Cataloging-in-Publication Data

The South Atlantic Coast and Piedmont / edited by Sara St. Antoine ;
illustrations by Trudy Nicholson. — 1st ed.
p. cm. — (Stories from where we live)
ISBN-13: 978-1-57131-664-6 (pbk. : alk. paper)
ISBN-10: 1-57131-664-7 (pbk. : alk. paper)
1. Piedmont (U.S. : Region)—Miscellanea—Juvenile literature. 2. Atlantic Coast (U.S.)—
Miscellanea—Juvenile literature. 3. Natural history—Piedmont (U.S. : Region)—Miscellanea—
Juvenile literature. 4. Natural history—Atlantic Coast (U.S.)—Miscellanea—Juvenile literature.
5. Piedmont (U.S. : Region)—Literary collections. 6. Atlantic Coast (U.S.)—Literary collec-
tions. 7. American literature—Piedmont (U.S. : Region) 8. American literature—Atlantic
Coast (U.S.) [1. Piedmont (U.S. : Region)—Literary collections. 2. Atlantic Coast (U.S.)—
Literary collections.] I. St. Antoine, Sara, 1966- II. Nicholson, Trudy H., ill. III. Series.
F217.P53S68 2004
975—dc22
                                                                                    2004005290

This book is printed on acid-free paper.

The South Atlantic Coast and Piedmont

Reapers and Sowers

Wild Lives

Appendixes: Ecology of the South Atlantic Coast and Piedmont

An Invitation

In the southeastern United States, stories are everywhere.

They're buried in the mucky peat of the Okefenokee Swamp, which retains a record of centuries of plant life.

They're inscribed in the rings of a one-hundred-and-fifty-year-old longleaf pine, which tell of wet years, dry years, and great searing fires.

They're tucked into riverbank fossils bearing the imprint of creatures that roamed the region millions of years ago.

They're bound up in the arrowheads, Civil War tags, and other historic artifacts that remind us of the communities that have come before ours.

And, of course, they're stored in the words, written and spoken, of people who have lived in this region for hundreds of years.

This anthology is a collection of stories from the land and people of the South Atlantic Coast and Piedmont. As you read them, you'll experience vicariously the excitement and diversity of the region. You'll tong for oysters on a Chesapeake fishing boat. You'll glimpse a pair of flying squirrels gliding overhead. You'll clamber up a backyard pine tree to return a great horned owlet to its nest. These stories may reveal new and surprising facets of the region to you. We hope they'll also inspire you to explore the region's life-filled hills and plains firsthand and make some fresh discoveries of your own.

The South Atlantic Coast and Piedmont ecoregion extends from Maryland south to Florida, and from the rolling foothills of the Appalachians to the pounding surf of the Atlantic Ocean. The western portion of this region is known as the Piedmont, a green, hilly swath of farms, cities, and forests. The eastern portion overlies the Atlantic coastal plain, a low-lying area filled with beaches, bottomland forests, swamps, marshes, and other habitats that have in many places been drained and tamed to make way for human settlements.

The South Atlantic Coast and Piedmont is home to the nation's capital, big cities such as Atlanta and Miami, and a rich variety of human cultural traditions. It's also awash with wading birds, songbirds, marine mammals, and more than a few moisture-loving reptiles. We've tried to capture both of these elements—the cultural and the ecological, and the ways in which they're linked—in the selections that make up the four parts of this anthology. In "Adventures" you'll read about kite-fliers, canoeists, fort-builders, and other people who have faced the elements in the great outdoors. In "Great Places" you'll venture to barrier beaches, longleaf pine forests, wet prairies, and even urban areas where people have discovered the presence of something rare and wild. In "Reapers and Sowers" you'll see how people both harvest from and care for the natural world, through activities such as digging for clams, collecting mushrooms, and cleaning up waterways. And finally, in "Wild Lives" you'll meet everything from a charming old raccoon to a ravenous crowd of alligators as you discover some of the many wild creatures that make this region home.

We hope you enjoy the poems, essays, and stories of this collection. Whether composed long ago or just this year, these stories have much to tell us about the South Atlantic Coast and Piedmont region and what makes it wondrous and unique.

—Sara St. Antoine

The South Atlantic Coast and Piedmont

Adventures

Anna's Tenth Summer

KATHERINE S. BALCH

If you've ever watched baby birds learn to fly, you may have noticed their hesitation, seeming self-doubt, and terrified cries for parental assistance. As Anna, the protagonist of this story, knows, freedom can be daunting— for birds and people alike.

Jumping off the swing, Anna walked to the edge of the bluff and looked down the length of her grandparents' dock.

She heard splashing near the inlet and saw three porpoises leaping in tight arcs, their backs shining white in the sun. They're having fun, she thought. The South Carolina air was thick with moisture, and the sun had thrown a cloak of heat from the east horizon right around to the west. The tide was dead low. Maybe it was napping before the ocean could sweep the salty water into the river again.

From inside the house she could hear her brother giggling. Grandma must be playing fisherman in the version of hide-and-seek she and Grandpa had invented. It was Peter's favorite game, one Anna had played over and over during the past winter in New York. "If I cast my line a little to the right, I just might catch that big red snapper," Grandma said teasingly. "Now, where is he? Peter, Peter, squeeter-eater, had a lie but couldn't keep her."

Anna's long brown hair stuck fast to her neck. With one hand swatting the mosquitoes that nibbled at her damp skin, she pulled her shorts loose from the backs of her legs.

Just a few minutes ago her mother had said, "You go on out and play. Grandpa will feed the baby." Her mother had reached for a clean diaper, and picking up the baby's feet, she'd slid the white rectangle beneath her round, pink bottom. "And Grandma and your dad will keep an eye on Peter, though a leash might be more effective."

Anna laughed reluctantly.

"Time you had some fun," her mother continued. "And some freedom."

Freedom. That's what she had been promised. Freedom from minding Peter for two whole weeks. Freedom to roam the woods around her grandparents' skinny shingled house, to lie in the hammock and watch the tide come in, to hunt for great blue herons among the marsh grass—all without an adult watching her. She was ten and a strong swimmer. The river was no longer a threat to her.

So why wasn't she already out exploring, she wondered as another of Peter's giggles interrupted her thoughts. What she wanted most, right now after a whole year away, was for Grandpa to come out and give her a good push on the swing. Or maybe Grandma could come out and help her make the bird feeder from the kit she'd brought from home. But they were too busy.

It didn't seem fair. It didn't seem fair at all.

The screen door banged closed, and Hitch, Grandpa's beagle, trotted over to her. She stroked his head and gazed out on the water, the light shimmering through the veil of misty heat. Hitch ran down the bluff along the path he'd carved out for himself over the years. He's probably headed for the mud, Anna thought. To cool off.

Among the palmettos and pines on the bluff, Anna spotted a streak of red. A cardinal? No, it was a red-winged blackbird. *OkaLEEEEEE. OkaLEEEEEE.* During his fourth trip between the marsh and the bluff, Anna looked more closely at the tree where he landed. In a little fist of branches, she could just make out a gray bird. It must be the mother.

Tcheee-tcheeeeee-tcheeeeeeee. A baby bird was nearby, but Anna couldn't find it until she moved one step to the left. There in the V of a branch was a small puff of gray. The father swooped down and back from the marsh again. The gray-speckled mother swooped down and back again. The baby just shivered.

Anna wondered if the mother and father were telling their fledgling how much fun it was going to be to hunt for mosquitoes all by himself. Or maybe they were telling him how beautiful the world looked from high above the trees. She was certain the baby's parents had no idea how tiny and fragile he felt, tucked inside his little corner of the world.

Wiping mosquitoes from her arms and legs as quietly as possible, Anna waited to see what the baby bird would do. Suddenly a dash of red appeared down on the dock, so far away that she had to make binoculars out of her hands to see better. Then she remembered. Peter was wearing a red shirt. But where was her father? And Grandma?

Her heart beating in her ears, she rushed to the window and yelled inside. "Peter's on the dock, Peter's on the dock!" She ran down the steps of the bluff, down the length of the dock, her heels pounding on the wooden planks, her eyes straining to see where Peter was. She reached the floating dock as he was leaning out over the water and grabbed his arm just in time.

"Fishy hide. Me find."

"Oh, Peter," she managed to say, panting after her long run. "Yes, fish play hide-and-seek, but you forgot to bring Grandma with you."

Their mother arrived only seconds later and swooped Peter into her arms. After hugging him so tightly her eyes closed, she put him down and placed her hands on his shoulders. "There's a big difference between a little fish who's born knowing how to swim and a little boy who's not." Mama explained about life jackets and lifeguards and living to the ripe old age of ten, when he could maybe, maybe, play by the river by himself. "Right, Anna?"

"Right, Mama."

Back at the house, sitting around the kitchen table, every-one was talking at once.

"I thought he was out here with you," Anna's father said to Grandma.

"And I thought he was in the bedroom with you, hiding from me." Grandma mixed sugar into the pitcher of lemon juice and water.

"He did come with me for a minute, but he kept saying, 'Dog, dog,' so I told him Hitch was in the kitchen with you and to go ahead." Her father scooped chocolate ice cream into cherry-colored bowls.

"Dog, dog?" Her mother wrinkled her brow and looked for a long minute at Peter. "No, he was saying, 'Dock, dock.' He was asking if he could hide on the dock, and when you said to go ahead, he thought you meant he could go on the dock. Well, thank goodness Anna knew exactly what to do. She's the hero of the day."

Anna asked for seconds on ice cream. When the cold sweet-ness froze the back of her throat, she paused to look around. Mama was taking a napkin out of the baby's mouth, Grandma was wiping off Peter's high chair, Daddy was changing Peter's diaper, and Grandpa was fixing something in his tackle box. When Anna's spoon failed to collect even one more drop of ice cream, she put the bowl on the floor for Hitch to lick. Everyone had something to do.

And so did she . . .

Outside, the leaves were fluttering and the river was rip-pling from the wind that always rode along with the incoming tide. The western sun was inking the blue water with puddles of red, orange, and purple.

OkaLEEEEEE. OkaLEEEEEE.

She glanced over at the branch where the baby blackbird had sat just an hour ago. It was empty. But skimming over the incoming water were one speck of red and two dots of gray.

Freedom.

Katherine S. Balch *writes from her home in Fanwood, New Jersey, and often longs for a South Carolina river sunset. She is the winner of the Society of Children's Book Writers and Illustrators 2001 Magazine Merit Award for Nonfiction.*

Summer of Being Ten

GRETCHEN FLETCHER

We were beaten
back and washed forth and beaten
back on rubber rafts
like so much summer flotsam
and jetsam
at the seam between sea and land
where the waves spit soap bubbles in arcs
along the sand,
and we said, "We could stay in the water
for the rest of our lives
and they could bring us hamburgers to eat and Cokes to drink."
"No. The whole ocean would be Coke,
and we could swim in it
and drink it too."
And the sun stung
our chicken-wing shoulder blades golden,
and our suits and all our
secret places
filled up with sand, and
out behind us streamed our mermaidens' hair in salty strands.

Gretchen Fletcher's *personal essays, travel articles, and poetry appear frequently in newspapers, literary journals, and anthologies. She leads writing workshops for the Florida Center for the Book and teaches fifth grade at a private school in Fort Lauderdale.*

Jack's Kite

GARY HENDERSON

Step outside in the South Atlantic Coast and Piedmont region in the early days of spring and you may find yourself buffeted about by strong, warm breezes. These breezes blow out the cold air, usher in flocks of migrating birds, and, of course, provide the perfect conditions for one popular pastime: flying a kite.

We seldom flew kites in my neighborhood, but one time we did on a spring afternoon in 1959 and it started a neighborhood party that lasted three nights and ended with the event being broadcast on the radio. It was late April. We'd had three Wednesdays of snow in March and were glad to feel the warm breezes. It was one of those days when you know winter has gone for good. Azaleas bloomed and the air felt warm, even when the wind gusted hard. It was a perfect day to fly a kite.

At first, there were only three of us. But as school buses brought home their loads, other kids headed to Rich Daniel's Grocery Store on the Asheville Highway for a ten-cent kite and a quarter ball of string. Soon, a half dozen colored kites flew in the skies over the north end of Spartanburg. "Let's put all the string on one kite," someone suggested. "There's no telling how high up we can get this thing to fly." Others joked about our kite joining Sputnik in orbit. The Russians were making big news with their space stuff then.

"We'll never get it back down," I said, letting the string slide through my hand as someone attached another ball of thin twine. The wind's tug on the string was gentle at first, but as the kite flew higher, it pulled hard. We took turns holding the string. After the string was all the way out, we could barely see the kite. It had become a tiny dot in the sky. "We'd better start bringing it in," I said. "It's getting dark."

Just as I said that, my dad walked up. "It's too bad you don't have a flashlight tied on the tail," he said with a chuckle. "Then you could see where it is."

That was all we needed to hear. I ran to my room and returned with a small penlight, the kind ushers used to show people to their seats in the crowded Carolina movie theater on Church Street.

"If this thing flies, it will be a miracle," I said, doubting it would ever leave the ground, but still rigging another kite to fly with a light. My dad was the pilot for liftoff. As he held onto the string, I walked to the middle of our front yard and faced the wind. The paper kite caught the wind and sailed toward the heavens.

"Dear God," said Jim Suttles as he watched the small light bounce around in the darkness. Jim was a truck driver. He lived two doors away and spent a lot of time sitting in his carport smoking cigarettes and drinking coffee. He kept a close eye on what happened on Pierpont Avenue Extension. "I always thought y'all was crazy," Jim said. "Now I know it. I never saw anybody fly a kite at night."

The news about our nocturnal kite flying spread quickly through the neighborhood. Soon, our driveway was full of people watching the light like it was a celestial beam sent down from the Almighty to glow on the north side of Spartanburg. Nobody could top this.

Then Jack Sparnell walked into the yard.

"If you had a bigger kite, you could get a bigger light up there," he said. "I'll show you how to really put something up there tomorrow night, when I get home from work."

Jack was always a lot of fun. He teased everybody and made us laugh. But the kite he carried into our front yard just before dark the following evening was no joke. It was huge. He had made the kite from a large piece of plastic my dad gave him from our basement.

Everybody stood back while he tied on a flashlight that held three fat D-cell batteries. Even more people came, but that wasn't surprising. The neighbors on our street were like that. Some of them were as close as family.

Again, there were good spring winds. And Jack performed the second miracle we'd seen in two nights. We were in awe as his kite pulled away into the darkness.

As we were eating supper the following night, the crowd started to show up again, though nothing had been planned. First the kids came, then the parents. It was our biggest crowd yet. Two kites with small flashlights tied onto the tails were already flying when I got outside. Nobody asked for permission to use our front yard again. They didn't have to. There were no fences on our street to separate the houses and the people. Property lines seemed unimportant. Several of the gathering crowd brought folding lawn chairs and transistor radios turned to WORD, the best rock 'n' roll station anywhere. The kites with the lights were what brought them. Gossip and good neighbors kept them there. Everybody was settling in for the evening.

Then Jack rolled up in his long, dark green sedan and parked along the side of the road. He was a mechanic at City Motor Car Company and worked on Dodges. But he drove a Pontiac. This thing he was driving was a four-door hardtop with a long hood and a trunk big enough to hide a Volkswagen.

Jack didn't say a word as he opened the trunk. He reached in and picked up one end of another of his creations. He had to twist and turn it from side to side just to get it out of the car. As he walked proudly into the driveway with his diamond-shaped monstrosity, I wondered if there was enough wind in all of Spartanburg County to fly it.

"Where'd you get that thing?" I asked him.

"I made it at work today," he said as he picked up a flashlight about the same size as a railroad lantern. "We're gonna light this place up tonight."

Jack had laid aside his work on the Dodges for the afternoon to make the kite. He was beginning to take this kite thing seriously. He'd used an old television antenna and brown paper to create a work of art.

"It'll never fly, Jack," someone scoffed. Jack never acknowledged the remark. He continued preparing for launch. Soon, the last knot was tied in the string that held the flashlight securely to the kite's tail.

"A couple of y'all take this over there and hold it up to the wind," Jack ordered.

I don't remember who helped me, but when we brought that monstrous thing upright, it filled with wind bound for Boiling Springs and it shot up like a mainsail.

"God Almighty," said Jim Suttles.

Jack pulled back on the string as the kite rushed upward.

Several people felt compelled to clap their hands. They stood amazed in the presence of the man who fixed Dodges.

Within minutes, the kite string was as tight as piano wire. The fat ball of twine flopped around on the gravel driveway in wild abandon. The string burned blisters on our hands as we took turns at the helm.

"Whatever you do, don't turn her loose," Jack said as we traded places while concentrating on keeping the string taut.

It was a strange sensation, piloting Jack's kite. Something seen only in the glow of a lantern light deep in the heavens pulled hard in our hands.

"What are y'all doing, watching UFOs?" said a man none of us knew as he got out of a white sedan he'd parked on the side of the road. As he closed the door I saw the words WORD MOBILE NEWS printed on the front door of the car.

"We've been getting calls at the radio station all night," the man said. "They say this is the third night UFOs have been flying around out here."

"Oh yeah, it's the third night we've seen 'em," Jim Suttles deadpanned. "We started to call you last night."

"Walk slowly to the backyard," Jack whispered to the other two kite fliers.

"I'm going to broadcast from right here," the man said as he reached in the car, stretched out a two-way microphone cord, and called the radio station. "We've got UFOs out here," the newsman said. "Put me on the air."

Of course Jim Suttles and Jack, who had returned to the front yard, were happy to be interviewed about the UFOs flying over the north end of Spartanburg. Neither of them had ever seen anything like it, they told the announcer, without the hint of a smile. This was serious business.

In the backyard, we continued to hold the kite string and tried to muffle our laughter as we listened to them on the transistor radio. But that was impossible, especially when Jim Suttles looked the newsman right in the eye and told all of Spartanburg, "This must be caused by that thing the Russians put in outer space."

Several other neighbors the man interviewed in our front yard spoke words of doom as well. All of them pretty much blamed the Russians for this awful event.

"I'll be back in just a few minutes," the announcer said, excitement building in his voice. "I'm going to drive over for a closer look, maybe get right under them. I'll be back on the radio from over there. I never saw anything like this!"

"Naw, none of us have either," said Fred Heatherly, who lived next door to Jim Suttles. "This is scary."

The radio man didn't respond. He slammed the car door and roared off in the direction of the UFOs that hovered over Boiling Springs Road.

"What a sight this is," he was telling radio listeners minutes after he drove away. "I am almost directly under the lights. Whatever these things are, they are not making noise. The lights are hovering high over an open field near California Avenue and Boiling Springs Road."

We laughed hysterically.

"Here comes the radio station man," a voice yelled from the darkness in the yard. "Now straighten up. No more laughing."

The newsman parked his Ford and got out. "This is really something," he said. "They're getting lots of calls at the radio station. I think I'll just stay here and watch to see what happens."

The kite fliers were trapped in the backyard, missing the fun that continued on the front side of the house.

"Get rid of that guy," Jack said finally, remembering the Dodges. "I have to work tomorrow. It's getting late."

Out front, they were still talking about how they'd never seen UFOs until this week. The small flashlights hanging on the tail of two kites had already gone out and the beam on Jack's beacon was fading.

"Well, it looks like they're all leaving," said the radio man as he walked to his car. "I guess I'll do another report and wrap this up."

Soon he was gone. The kite fliers came out of hiding and returned to the front yard.

"What a night," Jack said as he wound string around a stick of wood. "We made the news."

The two smaller kites came down quickly, but we had to take turns helping Jack get his monstrous kite back to earth. Finally, the kite was directly over our front yard. When the flashlight was low enough for me to reach it, I helped guide the kite down on the cool grass.

"We'll do it again sometime, maybe tomorrow night," Jack said as he opened the trunk lid on the Pontiac and put his kite back inside. The last of the crowd folded their chairs and walked toward home, still laughing about the newsman.

The next night, the winds that had put our kites in the air on three magic nights brought rain. By the time it quit a few days later, no one thought about the kites.

We never flew kites again after that spring night in 1959. I'm not sure why.

Years later, I was on the deck of a U.S. Navy ship in the Caribbean Sea. For the first time in my life, I saw a UFO. A large light bounced around in the sky for a long time. It was recorded in the ship's log as an unexplained event. A large crowd of sailors gathered on the port side of the ship to watch the glow in the western sky.

It reminded me of a spring night in my front yard in Spartanburg. And it made me wonder if Jack Sparnell was somewhere flying a kite with a long piece of string.

Gary Henderson *spent his childhood in Spartanburg. He moved west, eventually landing in Boulder, where he wrote stories for a Colorado magazine. He returned home in 1992 to write news and feature stories for the Spartanburg* Herald-Journal. *Gary is the co-founder of the Hub City Writers Project, a literary program that focuses on community and place. He is currently working on a collection of essays that follow his journey from the Carolina foothills to the Rockies and back home.*

Back of the Pack

SUSAN GRAY GOSE

The Chesapeake and Ohio Canal stretches for one hundred and eighty-four miles from Cumberland, Maryland, to Washington, D.C. Bikers, joggers, walkers, and nature lovers congregate on the twelve-foot-wide footpath that parallels the water. A plethora of flying, swimming, and creeping creatures share this peaceful corridor.

Today, I will keep up.

That's what Peg Holden told herself as she and the rest of the Potomac High cross-country team made their way to the C&O Canal in Washington, D.C. It was the start of their season, and today was their first hard run. It would prove who had trained over the summer and who had frittered about, who was fast and who was slow.

Moira, the team captain, was already picking up the pace. They hadn't even reached Coach Jerry Gruwoski, who was waiting for them under Key Bridge with a stopwatch to time the start of their six-mile run. This was meant to be a warm-up.

Everyone on the team envied Moira. She was five-foot-seven with long legs and straight red hair worn in a pixie cut like her idol, Lynn Jennings. She had a locker stacked high with coordinated running gear; even her socks matched her outfits.

Moira was fast. No one on the team, except Sissy, had ever beaten her. And the day Sissy beat Moira, Moira was recovering from mononucleosis.

As the girls approached Jerry—standing in the shadows of the bridge, bent at the knee—they lunged into a canter. "On your marks, get set . . ." The girls stormed by. "Go!" Jerry shouted.

A bicyclist stepped to the side of the dirt towpath to let the girls thunder past. Three Canada geese, sunning on the banks of the canal, took off and skidded across the water, straining their necks away from the commotion on the path. The canal's towpath was flat for the entire six miles; the pace would be unrelenting. The girls focused on the task ahead: run as fast as possible, beat as many teammates as possible. Peg glued her eyes to the back of Sissy's T-shirt, which read, "I'd rather be running." Peg had no doubt that was true.

I will keep up. I will keep up.

Peg's nickname on the team was Marcus II (or M-2), a name she wished they would drop. Marcus was her older brother. The famous Marcus. He had won the state championship as a senior, won the county race three years in a row, and left a trail of medals, honors, and press clippings in his wake. He had graduated two years ago, leaving behind the scent of his reputation in the school halls, it seemed to Peg.

Expectations were high when Peg joined the team as a freshman.

"Peg," Coach Jerry had said, pulling her aside at the team's first meeting in the gym. "I'm tickled you're joining the team. Your brother, Marcus . . . we're still mourning him. But I know you'll make us forget about him."

Peg just assumed she'd be fast. After all, she'd done well in the Presidential Physical Fitness runs in middle school. She even looked like Marcus: short and stocky with lemon-colored hair.

On the team's first hard workout last year, Peg had sprinted to the lead like a wild mare. Naturally, she should lead—though she knew nothing about pacing. By the start of the second mile, she was heaving in and out like a broken air pump. One after another, her teammates passed. It was as if Peg were jogging backward. The canopy of trees seemed to descend down on her. She'd never forget the feeling of reaching the third mile marker and wondering how she could possibly make it three more miles.

I will keep up. I will keep up. I will keep up.

On this run, Peg let the other girls lead. She'd learned her lesson last year. There were ten girls in all: the Fearsome Five-some, named for their top finishes in races, including Moira and Sissy, as well as Jasmine, Leah, and Adrienne; Sylvia, Ruth, and Judy, who played lacrosse in the spring and were insepa-rable friends; Shawn, "the Amazon," who was five-foot-nine and nearly 150 pounds; and, of course, Peg.

Peg felt good so far. Her breathing was steady; her legs churned rhythmically.

It was a beautiful fall day on the canal. Warm but breezy. Bikers and joggers sprinkled the path. Mallards paddled away from the canal's banks, leaving spreading ripples behind, as the girls passed. A painted turtle—with splashes of red and yel-low on its black shell—meandered along the grassy shoreline, ducking into its carapace as soon as the girls approached.

Maybe Peg would really keep up. Maybe this year would be

different from the year before when she'd finished in humiliating last place at the county race.

Afterward Peg had had to face Marcus, who was home for Thanksgiving break.

"You walked?" Marcus said, in horror, as Peg told her parents at the dinner table about her finish. Marcus leaned back in his chair with his hands clasped behind his head, looking as if he were the Sage of Running. Peg knew she was in for a lecture à la Marcus.

"Peg," he said, "you just need to get a handle on pain."

"Oh, that sounds like a formula for success," Mr. Holden said, giving his son a withering look.

"She just doesn't get it," Marcus said. "You can't expect to win and feel good. It doesn't work that way. You can't be a wimp."

"Marcus, really," said Mrs. Holden. She turned to Peg. "Dear, you play a very nice violin."

"Oh, Mom, please!" Peg pushed away from the table and fled to her room for refuge, but not before hearing Marcus add, "She's a girl, what can I say."

I will keep up. I will keep up.

As the girls passed the second mile marker, the pace remained quick. The team was spreading apart. Moira and Sissy were ten yards ahead of the pack. Peg ran in sixth place.

Peg was beginning to feel a strain in her legs and arms as she pumped them to maintain the pace. Just in front of her, Jasmine and Leah talked easily.

"So how many miles did you log this summer?" Jasmine asked.

"This summer? Three hundred. It would have been more,

but my family spent a week on a boat. My mom got mad when I tried to do laps on the deck. How about you?"

"Umm, three hundred sixty."

"You superhero!"

Peg realized she had no idea how many miles she'd logged over the summer. She hadn't kept track, but she was pretty sure it wasn't close to three hundred. And she wondered, How can they talk? Her breathing roared in and out. *I . . . can . . . barely . . . breathe . . .*

Peg felt like her insides had turned to lead; her rib cage and legs dragged at her as she drove her arms and legs forward. Her head buzzed as if a glaring fluorescent light had been turned on inside. Her mouth was parched. She felt an overwhelming desire to slow down. *Just a little slower so I . . . can . . . catch . . . my . . . breath,* she thought.

Shawn, who had been lumbering behind Peg, moved up beside her. She turned to Peg. "You okay, M-2?"

Peg cursed the nickname in her mind. "Yes . . . please . . . go . . . on."

Shawn gave Peg a doubtful look. But she said, "Okay," and galloped ahead to make up an opening gap between Peg and Jasmine and Leah.

As Peg's pace slowed, the trio of Sylvia, Ruth, and Judy—all running together—caught up to her and passed by, casting Peg a worried look. Judy shouted over her shoulder, "Come on, M-2, keep it up!"

But it was no use. Sluggishness was overcoming Peg. Tiredness crushed her competitive spirit. The girls shrank as Peg's pace continued to slow. A quietness descended around her. Her panting breath and thudding Nikes echoed in her ears.

As she passed the third mile marker, the girls disappeared around a curve in the path, and Peg was alone. Just like last year. She thought about the runs over the summer. The weekly five-mile workout around Washington's Tidal Basin. The invincible feeling she had some days bounding by the Jefferson Memorial and past the gnarled limbs of cherry trees. All for what? Here she was. Alone again. Plodding along as slow as ever. Nothing had changed.

Peg remembered the humiliation after last year's hard run of overhearing Moira and Sissy in the locker room. Peg was changing into her street clothes. Moira and Sissy combed their hair by the sinks.

"I thought she was going to be like her brother," Moira said.

"I know," said Sissy, Moira's best friend, who agreed with everything Moira said. "At least there's no chance she'll push our rankings down!"

Peg huddled by her locker until she knew they had left.

As the canal and towpath stretched out before her now—seemingly to infinity—Peg wondered why she bothered. She was no good. She didn't have Marcus's good genes.

"I'm like the mules that used to tug barges of coal on the canal," Peg thought. "Slow and lumpy."

Peg had learned about the mules from childhood walks on the towpath with her father. They took walks almost every Sunday with Polly, the family basset hound. Or sometimes, for a change, they rented a canoe and paddled down the Potomac River, which parallels the canal on the opposite side of the towpath. A biology professor, Mr. Holden pointed out the trees by name, teaching Peg how to tell them apart by their leaves and bark. He pointed out birds, including the noisy pileated woodpecker and the kingfisher that dove straight into the water in pursuit of a fish. And he talked about the history of the canal.

As she plodded along, Peg consoled herself: she was glad she knew these things. She doubted Moira and Sissy could tell a pawpaw tree from a sassafras. She looked at the trees in the thicket between the towpath and the Potomac. Pawpaws had elliptical leaves that fanned out in clusters, and warty brown bark. Sassafras leaves came in three shapes: one looked like a duck's webbed feet, another like a mitten, and a third like a petal. Peg was sure the other girls didn't know that sassafras roots smelled like root beer.

I will keep up. I will keep up.

As Peg neared the fourth mile marker, she tried to regain her focus. Just then, a great blue heron took off from a perch on a log and slowly, peacefully pumped its giant wings toward the treetops. The bird seemed to float on the air. The heron landed on the tip of an elm branch on the canal's opposite bank and watched Peg as she plodded by.

Despite her best efforts to concentrate on running, Peg couldn't help turning to look back at the bird. She waved hello, then felt foolish. She could hear Marcus say, "Are you a runner or a bird-watcher?"

But who could ignore a bird like that? Four feet tall with a beak like a spear and wings like a pterodactyl. On one of her canoe rides with her father, Peg remembered him resting his oars, looking up at the sky, and saying, almost to himself as much as to Peg, "Sometimes when I've worked too long at the office or spent too many hours in a committee meeting, I'll come out here and something small but great will happen. A fish will rise. A turtle will cross my path. A possum will peer down from a branch. And it's like . . . like . . . a wink from Mother Nature." He looked at Peg.

At the time, Peg didn't know what he meant. She'd rolled her eyes and said, "Get paddling, Dad."

But his words came back to her now. Running had always been a way to be outdoors and, on the best of runs, near nature. But the team competed so hard, Peg rarely had a chance to relish it. The trees, the birds, the frogs—all became a blurry backdrop to the running, jostling, and strategizing.

Peg looked up at the canopy of trees. "Maple," she said, spotting a familiar tree with jagged starlike leaves. She spotted elms, looming above all the others, with their zigzag branches. She saw a tulip tree with leaves that looked like faces wearing little crowns.

Maybe Peg would never be Marcus II. Maybe she was trying too hard to be like Moira and the others. She was Peg. Peg, the nature lover, the first chair in the school orchestra, the student singled out in art class for her landscape drawings.

And maybe she was also still Peg the runner, or at least the back-of-the-pack runner.

Despite her exhaustion, Peg smiled. She felt better. Just a little. Her breathing had steadied and her legs had relaxed.

What was that? A flash of blue from a pair of shorts appeared up ahead on the path, around the fifth mile marker. It was Shawn, who had fallen behind the others.

"No. I'll never catch her," Peg said to herself.

But she began to pump her arms harder and lift her knees higher, almost involuntarily. The trees' green mosaic of leaves rustled—as if they were fans in bleachers watching her dig her heels into the sandy path and lift off from her toes.

She was starting to feel good, like on the summer days on the Tidal Basin when she chased squirrels and pretended the cherry tree branches were trying to tag her. Her legs were churning smoothly. In comparison, Shawn's pace seemed sluggish.

While Peg was starting to feel strong, a pang of fear rose up. Was she going too fast? What if she choked and had to walk? Wouldn't that be worse than just reining in the pace now?

A wood duck paddled along the canal in tandem with Peg for a few yards before dropping off, craning his neck, and watching her move on. She imagined he was rooting for her to keep it up. She maintained her pace. And Shawn grew in size as Peg reeled her in. Every step brought the two closer together. Peg's breath was now coming fast and furious. But it wasn't a withering kind of breathing; it was a fighter's breath.

"I'm going to catch her," she thought. Her legs churned.

As Peg's breathing came within earshot of Shawn, Shawn turned to look at her, then drove her arms and legs faster.

Peg kept afoot with Shawn. Together the girls dashed toward Coach Jerry, holding out his stopwatch. "Forty-eight five, forty-eight six," he called out.

The two pumped their arms and sped toward their coach, lunging and crossing the line in unison.

"Forty-eight nine!" Coach Jerry yelled.

Forty-eight minutes and nine seconds. Peg stopped, bent over at the waist, grasped her knees with her hands, and heaved in and out, trying to catch her breath. Forty-eight minutes and nine seconds! She had never run six miles so fast.

"Good job, Peg," said Shawn, placing a weary hand on Peg's shoulder.

"You too," said Peg.

Jerry stood by the girls. "Good going, both of you." He waved his stopwatch in front of Peg. "Looks like your summer training paid off."

As the girls walked back to the team van, parked across a footbridge, they swabbed sweat from their foreheads, caught their breath, and rehashed the run.

"I was dead at the fourth mile marker," Adrienne proclaimed. "I thought, 'Two more miles? Oh, my gosh!'"

"I know," said Leah. "I felt like my legs were falling off. I felt horrible."

"I felt pretty good at that point," said Moira, pointing her toes like a ballerina stretching after her turn in the spotlight. "Actually, the whole run felt good."

"Ugh, I struggled just to keep you in sight, Moira!" Sissy said. "How do you do it?"

And on and on the conversation went as the girls piled into the van: sore muscles, gasping lungs, light-headedness, sprinting.

Peg smiled to herself. At the fourth mile marker, she had seen the great blue heron take off for the trees. At that point, the runner in the back of the pack had seen a wink from Mother Nature.

***

Susan Gray Gose *is a writer and journalist who lived in Washington, D.C., for ten years. A track competitor in high school and college, she has logged many miles on the Chesapeake and Ohio Canal towpath.*

On Assateague Island

CHARLES ROSSITER

we sipped
the late night
skinny
down
along
the open
coast
and wet
laid back
the stars
unzipped
the old
green tent
and then
there were
wild horses

Charles Rossiter *is an NEA fellowship recipient, Pushcart nominee, and host of the audio poetry Web site poetrypoetry.com. His chapbook,* What Men Talk About, *won the first Red Wheel Barrow Prize from Pudding Press. His book,* Back Beat, *traces in prose and poetry the ways in which he has been influenced by the Beats.*

Into the Okefenokee

C. W. DINGMAN

Alligators, bears, turtles, and wading birds are just a few of the hundreds of animals that inhabit Georgia's Okefenokee Swamp. The swamp's dense vegetation and hard-to-penetrate wetlands offer excellent shelter for wild creatures. But for humans, they can make travel tough going at just about any speed.

As parents with a great fondness for the outdoors, my wife and I always looked for opportunities to introduce our children to the joys of exploring the wilderness, an activity we both felt confident about undertaking. The chance to visit Disney World in Florida offered an inducement our three children couldn't resist. We would take them to see this world-renowned theme park if they would come canoe camping with us on the way to Florida. Skeptical though they were of the camping aspect of this proposed adventure, they ultimately agreed rather than risk not going at all.

I knew just the place for our canoe adventure: the Okefenokee Swamp. When I was young, I loved Walt Kelly's comic strip, *Pogo*, and ever since had harbored a strong desire to visit the Okefenokee Swamp where Pogo the possum, Albert the alligator, and all their animal friends supposedly lived. The swamp, which covers more than 400,000 acres in southern

Georgia, has been set aside as a national wildlife refuge. The plan seemed perfect. My wife, Noel, and I would get to see this great swamp firsthand and our children would experience an exciting two-night, three-day camping trip. Needless to say, the kids found it difficult to believe that spending two nights in a swamp could be anything but torture.

Following a night in a motel outside the Okefenokee, we set out in two canoes from the Suwannee Canal entrance on the eastern edge of the swamp. Our ten-year-old son, Stuart, and I paddled the lead canoe. Noel and our thirteen-year-old daughter, Sara, paddled the second canoe, and our younger son, Ross, age eight, sometimes rode as a passenger and sometimes took Sara's place paddling in the bow.

Although this first leg of our trip involved several hours of struggling against the current of the St. Mary's River, we took time to marvel at the many herons, egrets, snakes, anoles, and exotic carnivorous plants along the way. Our trail at this point was six to eight feet wide, bounded on either side by dense, six-foot-high bushes. We knew, however, that the river was wider than it seemed. The bushes here, as in most of this swamp, were growing not on solid ground but on floating masses of mud, mosses, and decaying vegetation. Getting out to walk was impossible.

By early afternoon we began looking for signs leading to our first night's campsite, which had been reserved on a floating island called Cedar Hammock. A tiny wordless sign on a post in the water bearing only an arrow pointing left seemed a promising clue. We turned left and paddled single file along a long, narrow trail cut through a more open prairie of short grasses

and low vegetation. When our canoes became stuck in the increasingly shallow water I got out, leaving the others behind, and walked several yards in the soft, oozing muck toward the dense and tangled vegetation of the hammock. Finding no evidence of a campsite, I assumed we were in the wrong place and returned to our canoes. Not yet discouraged, we paddled back out to the main trail and headed west.

After going several hundred more yards without seeing any other signs of a campsite, we began wondering if I'd failed to search well enough back at that unmarked hammock. My sense of having everything under control was beginning to wane. So back we went to that little side trail for a second attempt at finding our first night's destination. This time I walked farther through the mud and into the increasingly dense underbrush of the hammock but, once again, I found no helpful signs or anything resembling a campsite.

Reluctantly giving up the search, we returned to the main trail and again headed west. Our hope of finding our first night's campsite dwindled as the afternoon wore on and we proceeded deeper into the swamp. Perhaps, I thought out loud, we'd be able to make it as far as our second night's campsite.

My optimism soon faded as the trail became very narrow, overhung with vines and bushes, and obstructed by the protruding knobby "knees" of the cypress trees that shadowed our route. In one section we didn't even have enough room to use our paddles, and our canoes constantly became wedged between the bushes and the cypress knees. To make our way through this maze of vegetation, Stuart and I got out and waded in the swamp, each of us towing one of the canoes. Sometimes the water was calf deep and sometimes it was waist deep. Fortunately, we disturbed no cottonmouth moccasins, snapping turtles, or alligators along our passage, at least not any that we were aware of.

My show of optimism was by now only an attempt to keep Noel and the kids from getting upset and discouraged. But discouraged they were, and they soon began to doubt—out loud—that I knew what I was doing. Our fascination with the plants and animals around us gave way to increasing anxiety about how and where we'd be spending the night. The scary thought that we might really be lost was left unspoken.

Fortunately, by late afternoon the trail became wider and easier to navigate. The sun, however, was now sinking rapidly toward the horizon and our arms and shoulders ached from paddling. We'd gone well over twelve miles since morning without a clear sign of a campsite anywhere along our route. And hunger and fatigue were taking their toll.

With the sun finally setting and with no sign of our campsite, we paddled our canoes off the trail into the thick lily pads so they wouldn't drift in the wind and current, and then lashed them together for stability. We were none too soon. In the dimming light the mosquitoes descended on us in thick swarms. Quickly consuming any food we had that didn't need cooking, we dressed ourselves completely in plastic garbage bags, hoping to rob those voracious insects of access to anything but our noses.

Very uncomfortable and very unhappy, the kids began to complain loudly. Sara announced her certainty that we'd never get out of the swamp at all. In their view, we'd proved ourselves quite incompetent as wilderness guides. I had to admit that sleeping in cramped canoes with our camping gear was certainly far more roughing it than their mother and I had anticipated. Listening to the two of us sing "On Top of Old

Smoky" and "The Big Rock Candy Mountain" did nothing to improve their mood. They had no trouble seeing through our feeble attempt to pretend that all was well.

As night descended, a flashlight survey of our surroundings revealed the large, bright, reflective eyes of both a multitude of grunting pig frogs and many close-in curious alligators who serenaded us with their mating calls. "Alligators all around," commented Noel dryly, trying to make light of her own concerns. We couldn't, of course, leave the canoes that night, so bathroom functions had to be taken care of by leaning awkwardly over the side. In an uncomfortable, folded position with my head on the point of the canoe's stern, I did not sleep. Instead, I watched the Big Dipper rotate ever so slowly around the North Star.

The colorful dawning of the new day, accompanied by the singing of numerous birds and a chorus of frog sounds, was something only Noel and I could appreciate. Hungry for a real breakfast and still groggy from lack of sleep, we set out once again. Relief and delight were quickly ours: Floyd's Island, where we'd been scheduled to spend our second night, was but a few hundred yards beyond our canoe camp.

Thankfully, the warm air, the intriguing, junglelike vegetation of this sandy island, and the opportunity to stretch our legs after the confinement of the canoes soon began to soothe our tired bodies and calm our frayed nerves. Noel and I—not ones to miss an opportunity for more adventure—immediately proposed spending the day exploring the island's dense, subtropical woods. With some reluctance and understandable skepticism, the kids agreed to tag along.

Our early morning wanderings into the island's lush vegetation startled a tiny newborn fawn who'd been hidden by her mother under a bush. And the fawn then startled us by emerging suddenly from the vegetation just a few feet in front of us. The sight of her bright white spots gleaming in the sunlight as she raced away to find another hiding place put smiles on all our faces. Later that day, as we entered a small clearing in the woods, we were greeted by the friendly hooting of a curious barred owl watching us intently from the limb of a sweet gum tree. He seemed not the least bit afraid of us. To each of our clumsy attempts to mimic his call he responded with another series of his eight syncopated hoots, as if trying hard to teach us to say it right.

That afternoon, the boys—by now feeling more accepting of their parents and willing to forgive us our ineptitude of the previous day—amused themselves by climbing up onto the large limbs of a great live oak. There they perched, several feet above our heads, glowering and chattering at us like scolding monkeys in some faraway tropical rain forest. They were the only animals we sighted in those heavily shaded woods that would sit still long enough for us to get a picture!

These experiences helped us all regain our sense of humor and rekindled our enjoyment and awe of the many sights and sounds of this magnificent wildlife refuge. Fortunately, the canoe trip back to the Suwannee Canal entrance the next day went smoothly and did no further damage to our children's estimation of their parents' competence as wilderness guides.

Although we never returned to the Okefenokee as a family, Noel and I went back by ourselves the following year and spent five days and nights on a circular canoe trip through the middle of the swamp. The trip was, fortunately, free of any mishaps. And to this day, the Okefenokee remains one of the most fascinating places we've visited, as well as the site of an adventure none of us will ever forget.

***

C. W. Dingman *has begun to write articles and stories for children after careers in basic science and psychiatry. He and Noel remain avid outdoor enthusiasts and continue to enjoy vacationing in wild and remote places, while Sara, Stuart, and Ross, now grown, live adventures of their own making.*

A Peek

McCabe Coolidge

this nursery where
wild things roost
me too on canoe
I paddle, wiggle in and out
sniffing along like a dog
canvassing a row of bushes

I'm enchanted among these
neighbors, webbed feet,
overcoming water's density
they lead me out the channel

coot and grebe, an entourage
they, like tugs, me the green boat
they, spawning small wake
me following their crossing
leaning into paddle, pitching
deep into dark density

the coot can dive plus walk on water
I chuckle as I follow them,
finding a way through loneliness

coiling, like a rope, my destiny
to theirs

my inner being realigned, calmed
lazily, my canoe rafts in rhythm
to these oily feathered birds who
in this estuary where I live
call me down, as if I too
can just sit here, letting currents
flow, they offer me hope that
even I can come alive in the drifting

McCabe Coolidge *lives along the Outer Banks of North Carolina, where he writes essays and poems about endangered species, homelessness, life on two uninhabited islands, love, and loss.*

The Fort

KIMBERLY GREENE ANGLE

Anyone who has ever built a fort knows of the satisfactions they provide: the comfort of shelter, the power of creation, and the sense of a small but personal claim upon a very large world. Kimberly Greene Angle experienced all this and more at the age of nine when she built her first fort near her Georgia home.

"I'm scared, Kim," Lydia said in the darkness.

In response to her voice, a hoot owl called out from deep in the woods.

I looked out the side door of our fort to see the full moon glancing white off the lake. I could understand why Lydia was scared, but I wasn't, really. My nose itched from the must that rose from the forest floor at night, and I felt damp and uncomfortable. But I knew I didn't want to leave. Lydia and I were nine years old, after all. We had become official best friends that summer and built our first real fort. Now we'd made it past midnight in the woods. To go back would be the worst kind of defeat.

"Everything's fine, Lydia," I said to reassure her. "Sam's right here, and his eyes are open. You know he'd bark his head off if anything were wrong."

Sam was my black lab. His tail thumped the ground when

I said his name. He was curled up on the leafy floor of the forest and staring at me with his droopy eyes as if he, too, were willing me to go home. I was trying my best to ignore him. Spending the whole night in the fort was to be the crowning achievement of our summer. We had to stay.

"I'll keep watch for a while," I told Lydia. "You go back to sleep."

Lydia sighed and pulled her sleeping bag up tighter around her neck. It wasn't long before I heard her breath grow lightly measured, with an occasional whiffling noise. She had fallen back asleep.

Unconsciously, I patted the ground behind me where we'd buried our storehouse of canned goods. Lydia and I had decided that we would be ready if the Russians ever attacked Atlanta. We'd filched pork and beans, Campbell's soup, and even a six-pack of Coke from our homes. We'd also sneaked a few cans of corn from my grandmother's cupboard. It wasn't really stealing because it was for everyone's own good. If a bomb ever hit and the Russians invaded, we would bring our families here to our fort. Here is where we would survive.

I didn't mind keeping watch during the night. I'd already stayed awake long enough to hear the evening call of the whip-poor-will. And long enough to notice how the incessant chatter of the katydids and tree frogs grew louder with the height of the moon. Every once in a while I saw a shadow move, and I wondered if the woods were indeed haunted by the ghost of a Cherokee that once lived in these foothills. Or if the old cedar were haunted by the ghost of a slave. If I'd been a slave, or if I'd been taken from my land, I know I'd come back to haunt. But after the shadows moved, everything was still.

Then I watched the lightning bugs retreat higher into the

trees, as if the bugs were trying to follow the path of the moon and play with the stars.

No, I didn't mind being awake. In fact, I hadn't been sleeping much lately anyway. Ever since the summer started, I'd noticed that my parents had started arguing. At night. A lot. And what was really frightening was that in the morning everyone acted as if nothing had happened.

I didn't tell Lydia that I was much more scared to go home than to stay in the woods all night. I was scared of her seeing my family fall apart.

We had built the fort in early June, starting at my grandparents' house. My grandparents lived just down the road, and their land connected to our twenty acres. Before we left that morning, my grandmother fed us a breakfast of fried eggs, bacon, and grits.

"Chiggers," my grandmother had said as I scraped the last bit of grits from my plate. "Chiggers and poison ivy and ticks. That's all will come of a day in the woods."

Lydia and I submitted to being saturated with Off!, but we were steely in our resolve. We were on a mission, and would not be scared away by my grandmother's warnings.

Our first stop was my granddad's tool shed.

"Rome wasn't built in a day," my granddad said as we burst into the dimness of his shed. He often said this when he saw me intent on a task.

We smiled and rummaged through some old tomato baskets for a ball of bale-binding twine. I loved the tool shed. A coolness always lingered there, even in the dog days of August. An old white icebox sat in the corner, promising the treat of a cold slice of watermelon in the evening. And I loved the smell of the place—its odor was part oil, part cut grass, part old TVs; it smelled metallic, yet alive, like some strange mechanical plant grew there.

After we gathered our supplies, Lydia and I bade Granddad good-bye and struck out across the fields where the strawberries and golden broom sedge grew. We made our way through a tangle of kudzu to the pine thicket where the trees stood as straight and thick as soldiers. We were heading to the hardwoods where oaks and maples, hickory and cypress made a huge canopy of green. Our final destination was an outcropping of granite rock beside the lake. We knew this was the same type of rock as Stone Mountain near Atlanta, which we had climbed together.

When we reached the lake, we spread our possessions on the cool, flat surface of the rock: binding twine, a few rusty nails, an old hammer, the little brown lunch bags of oatmeal creme pies my grandmother had supplied us with, and a shiny aluminum thermos of milk.

The sun was winking golden on the lake already, but we knew we had plenty of time to build our Rome. We'd discovered that in the summer there was always time enough. Time to see the blue of the sky. Time to follow the rap-tapping of a woodpecker to the standing dead tree where it lived. Time to watch the turtles climb out of the lake onto a log and then plop back in again. We knew that the blue sky would stretch long enough for us once again that day.

The granite ledge was the perfect place for us to begin. We'd known about it for years, and I'd always imagined that the Cherokee used it for shelter as well. If we crouched down, we could find adequate shelter from the rain.

"Kim, you don't think there's snakes under there, do ya?"

Lydia said as we started digging into the hill to make more room under the ledge.

"No." I didn't tell her that there probably were. But I respected the animals and gave them space, and they never bothered me. I figured this formula would keep holding true.

We used crude rocks and sticks, and even our hands to dig out our space. As we dug, the soft, orange clay packed into tight c's under our fingernails.

Next we embarked on our search for the main support beam. We were fortunate to find a large, freshly fallen oak. It took both of us using all our strength, but we managed to hoist it up and cradle it between two trees growing against the rock. With this accomplished, we wiped the sweat from our brows and sat down to eat our oatmeal pies. We thought we'd worked hard enough to deserve our treat. Sam came back from his exploration of the banks of the lake to enjoy one too.

As we ate, Lydia and I surveyed our oak log with pride. We'd both been involved in fort building for a while. We'd been part of other kids' fort projects, and I'd helped with the finishing touches of my big brother's forts several times. Lydia and I had even tried a few forts on our own. But they'd always been flimsy, slipshod affairs that collapsed in a few days. Now we understood that our main support beam was our fort's true foundation. We'd learned that a fort is built from the sky down.

We soon finished our treat and went back to the task at hand.

After a while, I said, "I think Einstein built a fort over in Germany when he was a kid."

"You do?" Lydia asked as she balanced a pine branch on the main beam for our wall. We'd been canvassing the woods and had gone as far back as the pine thicket to find branches of the right length and thickness.

"Well, think about it," I said. "He dropped out of school, so he probably had a lot of time on his hands." I really didn't know that much about Einstein, but I'd seen a textbook picture of him at school, and I liked his shock of white hair, his walrus mustache, and his droopy eyes.

I placed one more log on the support, and all the others fell down like dominoes.

"Uh-oh," I said.

But Lydia was laughing. "I bet Einstein never did anything like that," she said.

When we started again, we reinforced each beam of our wall more tightly with the binding twine. As the sun grew level and started to pick out bright peach and pink tones in the horizon, our wall was solid and secure.

For finishing touches we collected some fresh sun-baked pine straw and spread it for a carpet over our clay floor. Then we went to search for oak leaves. I'd watched squirrels all my life, and I knew the kind of leaves they collected when they were nesting. They sought out the leaves that look like little leathery hands. These particular oak leaves stay on the trees all winter. During that time they age against the elements and grow as shiny and resilient as plastic. Lydia and I used these leaves to cover our fort for extra protection and for camouflage. Disguising our fort was important, we knew. If a secret fort were discovered, it was the protocol of the woods that it be destroyed.

By the time we placed the last oak leaf on the wall, the evening geese were returning to bed down at the lake, and the crickets and frogs had started their evening chorus. We'd been right: the blue of the sky had stretched long enough for us to build our Rome. Our fort was complete.

From that day on, Lydia and I spent as much time as possible at our fort. Some days it was our camp. Some days it served as a makeshift church for us—a place for us to say the Lord's Prayer and sing "Fairest Lord Jesus" and "Amazing Grace." It just as easily became a rustic library when we brought out our Nancy Drew mysteries and Archie comic books. Sometimes it was just our quiet place. But it was always a refuge somehow from the rest of our lives. It was the first structure we'd built with our hands. The first spot of earth we could claim as our own.

One day I'd come to the fort without Lydia. Just with Sam. I hadn't told Lydia about that day because talking about what was happening would have made it too real. It had been a bad day. My parents had been arguing, and I heard them yell the dreaded word, the "d" word. Divorce.

My response was to flee immediately. To escape the word.

I slammed the screen door open and ran out into the yard with Sam at my heels. Even before I reached the fields, my breath was coming quickly and building to sobs. But I fought back the tears with all my might and ran harder. My legs were pumping faster and faster, my hands punching at the air, pulling me forward. My lungs gasped for air. Sam soon overtook my sprint. But I raced after him. I ran with everything I had so that I could be pure motion, motion with no feeling. I ran and ran until I arrived at the fort.

I was sweating, but I still wanted to be in the sunlight.

I needed warmth. I looked up at the summer sky. I didn't understand how it could be so blue when I felt so much pain.

Now, as I stood at the edge of the fort, the sky was almost black, except for the white eye of the moon. But I was still having a hard time understanding.

Sam shifted his two front paws, still intent in his droopy-eyed stare, as if he could read my thoughts.

The night was beginning to feel endless, and I was exhausted. With an enormous yawn, I crawled back into the fort and nestled down in my sleeping bag next to Lydia. But, before I fell asleep, I vowed to tell her about my parents. I realized now that I needed her to know.

Pink tongue and black fur greeted me in the morning. While Sam was assaulting me with his mouth, his tail was whapping at Lydia's face. I heard her groan, and I laughed out loud. Then I opened my eyes to the brightness of the morning in the woods and realized the full significance of the sun. We had stayed in the fort for an entire night on our own!

"Lydia," I yelled. "Wake up! It's morning! We survived the night!"

Lydia poked her head out of the sleeping bag, gave a yawning grin, and simply said, "Thank God."

We were grimy and starving for a big breakfast. Sam had gulped down our peanut butter and jelly sandwiches the evening before, and we'd been left to delve into the "fallout" store for a can of pork and beans with freshly picked strawberries for dessert.

But, despite our hunger, we were triumphant. We were nine

years old, we were best friends, and we had spent the whole night in the woods.

Kimberly Greene Angle *and her best friend Lydia did get chiggers, poison ivy, and ticks when they built their fort. But they submitted to the tomato juice and salt tinctures administered by Kimberly's grandmother, with gritted teeth and the steely resolve that this small amount of suffering was worth all they had accomplished under the blue sky of a Georgia summer. A published writer, Angle shares her life with her husband and two small children in Columbia, South Carolina.*

Breathless Toes

APRIL PULLEY SAYRE

A winter's smile
gleams through
the hasty chilled
hot chocolate days
as we wait for that
fresh delicious moment:
barefoot day!
in which to run—
feeling crisp new grass
between our long-lonely toes
training our tender feet while
turning exuberant cartwheels
drinking peppermint ice cream air
leaving leather shoes
far behind.

April Pulley Sayre *grew up in Greenville, South Carolina. She wrote this poem when she was fourteen years old. She is the author of such books as* Secrets of Sound *and* Crocodile Listens.

Chesapeake Homeplace

SUSAN SCHMIDT

Some people are born adventurous—always seeking new experiences and new thrills. But many successful adventurers have had a wise mentor, someone who has given them the skills, judgment, and confidence to reckon safely with the elements. For Susan Schmidt, that person was her father, one of a long line of Chesapeake sailors.

When I was young, my daddy told me he was once a little girl and had kissed his elbow to become a boy. In a photo at the age of five, he wears a white lace smock, black leather boots mid-calf, and long blond ringlets. So I believed him. I tried and tried to kiss my own elbow, bending and twisting my arm, jutting my chin over or under, to no avail. When I was five, my daddy's golfing buddies would ask me, "Who are you like?" and I'd answer, "Jess like my daddy." Like my daddy, I loved boats and I loved the water, and I didn't have to be a boy for that.

I grew up by Virginia's Chesapeake Bay, as my father had. I remember his stories as clearly as my own childhood. As a boy he helped load a farmer's watermelons on a bugeye bound for Baltimore. On this ancient sailing workboat, with a one-lung engine for auxiliary power, the grand canvas sail was wrapped on the boom that extended way over the stern, ready to unfurl if the engine broke down. When my father was thirsty on a hot summer day, he would drop a watermelon, grab a fistful of red, sweet heart-meat, and kick the rest off the dock. Eating just the heart of watermelon is as rich as I can imagine. As a young man Daddy raced sailboats on the Bay. Once before the war, his wooden sailboat opened a seam and sank off Stingray Point. He told me, "I had to stay afloat all night with jellyfish up my pants leg," a story that still makes my skin crawl.

I spent my first summers at our river cottage on Jackson Creek on Coles Neck, which is on the southern shore of the Potomac River, and I went to school in Richmond living right by the James River. As early as I can remember, I waded the creek, happy to be wet. I could swim almost as soon as I could walk. At two I waded the shallows by a marsh with a big grin and mud oozing from both fists. At three I leaned over the gunnel of a white, wood deadrise skiff while Daddy was fishing. In family albums I always appear in a bathing suit.

As soon as I could swim, I was allowed in a boat alone. My first journeys were floating in the heavy wooden skiff tethered to the shore. No matter the distance, being afloat was what mattered. I could pull myself back to land by the rope. At the age of stubby pigtails, I rowed a featherweight dinghy to the limits of our cove—far enough to taste adventure, but close enough that a parent could look out a window and see me. If I shipped the oars and made no noise floating, I could see lots of birds and animals along the shoreline. The kingfishers scolded me as they swooped between pine branches, and the great blue heron squawked if she was stalking fish. I counted baby goslings swimming tight in line behind their goose

mother. Mid-
cove, mute
swans were
ornery despite
their white beauty,
and I stayed clear of
them. I picked up their white wispy feathers floating
on the water surface. If I were really quiet, I might glimpse
a shy otter on the shore, or see just its dark head bob underwater. I always hoped a jumping mullet fish would land in my
boat.

My father introduced me to other wild residents of the
creek. On the sandy shore by the lapping water, he taught me
to whistle the three-part bobwhite call, *wher-wher-it*. From my
bedroom window I'd lean halfway out, with him anchoring
me inside, as I whistled and listened to the bobwhite's response, over and over. On the hottest nights, I fell asleep to
whip-poor-wills, bullfrogs, and tree toads. If I woke, I could
hear the wind blowing in the pine trees all night long.

Our creek, mid-salinity halfway up the Bay, was also perfect
for blue crabs and oysters. On summer evenings, Daddy
steamed trash cans
full of crabs that
turned from

blue to red. *Callinectes sapidus,* the blue crab, means beautiful swimmer that tastes good. Before I was six, I could pick a crab clean, pulling off the legs, ripping away the underbelly skirt (different for males and females), scooping inedible gills and "deadmen," breaking the white shell body in half, and fingering out gobs of backfin meat. We smoked bluefish in the old metal refrigerator. Whoever cranked the peach ice cream in the cedar bucket got to lick the paddle. In the fall we roasted oysters on metal grates over driftwood fires, so the shell would pop just enough to slide a knife in the slit.

Boating became a real bond for my father and me. Rising early, Daddy and I went fishing with his cronies for blues and stripers in the middle of the Bay, in hot sun all day with no shade. The old men told stories, and I listened or daydreamed. Lunch was lemonade from a Ball jar and baloney on white bread. My father baited my hook and pulled off my tiny spot or croaker, until I caught so many that I had to bait my own hook. Summer afternoons, when clouds darkened the sky and thunder boomed far off, we motored back in, docking just before lightning and pelting rain. I always felt secure with my father because the rain never seemed to catch us.

I followed my father when he looked at sailboats and talked to yachtsmen and fishermen. I kept up, even though my knees shook, on a waterman's rickety dock stretching precariously over marshland to the water's edge, its shaky or missing boards alternating with solid ones. Once, I leaned under a dock to see what was swimming by and stuck my face right into a nest of wasps that swarmed in my face. Not one bit me before my father whisked me away to safety.

When I was ten, my father built a sailfish from a plywood kit on the living room floor, while my mother complained about the smell of paint and varnish in the house. My father could lift the seventeen-foot sailfish and carry it on top of his car. When we launched the boat in the creek, my father yelled from shore, advising me to *point*, or sail as close to the wind as I could, and to lean on the high windward side. He told me to loosen the sheet so the sail would spill air, to push the tiller leeward so the boat would *fall off* the wind. I learned to balance these three forces—the sheet, the tiller, and my weight leaning back—as my toes tucked under the varnished rail. When I was not quick enough in a gust to spill wind out of the sail, the boat capsized. With stinging jellyfish in the creek, I did not want to be in the water for long. No problem: I swam underwater clear of the lines and the red-and-white striped sail. I jumped on the centerboard to right the boat, grabbed the tiller and sheet, and took off again in the wind.

That summer I begged my mother to cut off my braids, which were halfway down my back. She saved them in a box tied with a ribbon. My curly short hair now dried as quickly as my nylon bathing suit.

After I learned about tacking in the wind on the sailfish, my father trusted me steering his thirty-five-foot sailboat when we cruised on the Chesapeake Bay for two weeks every summer. I could follow a course on the compass. I knew, for example, that heading due east means ninety degrees. In reading channel markers, I knew "red right returning" means leaving a red buoy on the right entering a harbor and a green one on the left. We had to stay in the channel because Daddy's sail-boat had a keel five feet deep.

That August, right before school started, we were sailing on the Miles River approaching St. Michael's on the Eastern Shore. A white signpost stood in the water and I steered closer to read its message. When we were near enough to read "SHOAL," the sailboat went aground on the sand bottom. We dropped the sails, and as the tide went out, the sailboat leaned way over on its keel. We didn't know until the tide came back in if high tide would be high enough, or if we'd have to radio for a tow. My brother teased me, and I felt guilty for a minute, but my fa-ther laughed and said I was learning by experience. The four of us—my mother, father, brother, and I—took turns choosing classical or rock 'n' roll stations on the radio. On that very hot, very long afternoon we alternated listening to Mozart, Elvis, and the Drifters as thunder rumbled in the distance. When the tide came in again, the boat finally floated off the sandbar so we could sail away before the storm hit. We reached St. Michael's to anchor just before dark.

The next day, we sailed five hours across the Chesapeake Bay to Annapolis in fog and driving rain. I guess my father had to get back to work, or we had to start school. In zero visibility we crossed Eastern Bay, renowned for monster jellyfish, into a fleet of sailboats racing from Annapolis to St. Michael's. I stood watch while my father steered, but I couldn't see any dis-tance ahead. Big white sails emerged ghostly from the fog, and Daddy weaved between the racing boats, which held their course.

My father never let me know if he was frightened. What did he think about that time his sailboat sank? He always told that story of floating all night with jellyfish as humorous instead of dangerous. As a Coast Guard commander in World War II he had driven ships around the world, so sailing into the fog crossing the Bay could not have seemed too dangerous. And because he didn't seem afraid, I was steady.

What my father taught me about boats when I was a little girl has stayed with me my whole life. After I finished college and taught for a dozen years, I got a captain's license and delivered sailboats from the Chesapeake Bay to the West Indies. Once I sailed ten days across the ocean in fifty-mile-an-hour winds and twenty-foot waves. At sea, if strong winds or high waves ever scare me, or in tough situations on land, I am confident because my father taught me to navigate. Even if I feel a little fear, I know that is good, too, because it reminds me to be cautious.

Growing up, before my father gave me permission to do something, I would tell him three reasons why I should and three reasons why I shouldn't, so I could learn how to make decisions on my own when he wasn't around. Sailing with my father and later in boats on my own, I have learned judgment and responsibility. He allowed me to row within the limits of our cove and then encouraged me to sail alone in a boat. In so doing, he gave me the freedom and confidence to explore the world.

In 2002, **Susan Schmidt** *circled the Chesapeake Bay in a small boat, following Captain John Smith's 1608 voyage. She is writing a book about John Smith, Chesapeake ecology, and her adventures before the 400th Commemoration at Jamestown. A grant writer, technical editor, and naturalist, Schmidt has won grants and awards for her nature essays. She teaches English at Carteret Community College in Morehead City, North Carolina.*

Great Places

Oystercatchers on the Moon

Joe Shepherd

Camouflage provides security for many animals that live along the South Atlantic coast, from dun-colored spider crabs that creep along the sandy ocean floor, to bitterns with thin brown stripes like stalks of cattails, to spotted fawns hiding in the dappled forest light. But what happens to residents, human and wild, if they just don't blend in?

It was not a postcard day. This was good news to Lily. It meant no one would be on the beach to bug her. It was only March, so not many tourists would be around anyway, but they definitely wouldn't be here on a day like this. The mist had hung on all day, clinging to the shore and marsh, rubbing out the line between the ocean and the sky. Lily liked that, too. She liked to stand at the edge of the surf and imagine bending her knees and springing into the air, up and away from this place. On days like today, when the air and water seemed one big open space, it made her little fantasy seem that much more possible.

Assateague Island is a place of sun-bleached browns and faded greens. This day, the low, sticky sky overflowed with clouds in a hundred shades of gray. The only bright color to be seen was the Day-Glo orange on the stripes of Lily's shoes. The sunlight was like a lamp behind a thick curtain. Lily squinted through the haze as she looked out across the water and sand.

The gusting breeze blew off the marsh behind her, scattering strands of black hair across her face and into her eyes. There was nothing special about those eyes. They were shaped like her mother's, colored like her father's. But they had attracted a lot of attention over the years. Other kids thought Lily's eyes were strange.

Most of the time she could handle the stupid things some of the kids said at school. But by the end of the long, cooped-up winter, Lily had usually had all she could take of the whispered comments in the hall and the nicknames like Dragon Girl. So this was the worst time of year for Lily: that never-ending stretch between the last day of spring break and the first day of summer vacation. Not that she hated school itself. Straight-A report cards and lots of yearly award certificates were tucked away in Mom's desk at home. It was just all those other *people* who were the problem. They were the ones who made the slow trudge toward June so tough. They were the reason for Lily's frequent escapes to this sandy edge of the world.

Lily Chen's parents had immigrated to Ocean City, Maryland, a few years before she was born. Relatives who had come before had offered them a place to live and work and had promised an easy transition to American life. No promises were made about raising an American-born daughter who would grow up smart and restless, though. And the Delmarva Peninsula was no place to be restless. Named for the three states that share the flat expanse of land—Delaware, Maryland, and Virginia—the Eastern Shore, as most people call it, is home to people who take great pride in preserving a simple, older way of life. At least that was what the travel brochures said. To Lily, it was equal parts tourist trap and time capsule. It was a place of old fishing towns and farms, a place where families traced their ancestors back to the exact boat that brought them over from Europe. Generations lived and died here without moving more than a few miles from the original settlements of their long-dead relatives. To a twelve-year-old kid whose ancestors came over on a 747 instead of a three-masted sailing ship, it was proof that this was not where she belonged.

Quiet fishing towns and farmland weren't the only features of Delmarva. In fact, what really brought the tourists running from Washington, D.C., was Ocean City. They came by the millions all summer long to this long narrow strip of high-rise hotels, souvenir shops, and miniature golf courses. Lily never understood why stressed-out families drove four hours to sit on the beach in crowds bigger than the ones they left behind in the city, but she kept her mouth shut about it around her parents. After all, those people and their money were more than welcome at her parents' restaurant in the heart of the Ocean City strip. So she came here instead, just a few miles down the coast but worlds away from high-rises and schoolmates, to talk to the wind and the water when her world made no sense. And it made no sense most of the time lately.

"That's just part of being twelve years old," her mom had said one day. "It's true all over the world. In China, in United States—probably even for twelve-year-olds on the moon!" she laughed.

Thanks for the pep talk, Mom, Lily thought sarcastically.

While her father lingered near the ranger station reading the *Washington Post*, Lily slowly snaked her way down the beach. First she wandered along the marsh side, slogging through the loose, shifting sand. Small brown birds appeared and disappeared among the faded marsh grasses, their intricate patterns of stripes and spots helping them hide from harrier hawks that patrolled the marsh like low-flying hang gliders. Then she walked along the ocean side, where the receding tide had left the sand sidewalk-smooth and hard. There were birds here too. But they were different in shape and movement. Running in and out with the waves, shorebirds poked and prodded the sand for aquatic insects and other buried treats.

Then a flash of color caught Lily's eye and she stopped. A wave ran up the sand and over her shoes, but Lily didn't notice. She was concentrating on a strange bird strutting around a small pile of driftwood covered in brown seaweed. She had been to this beach a hundred times before, but she had never seen this bird. She was sure of it. It would be impossible to forget. Its shape and sand-poking feeding method told Lily it was a shorebird, but bigger than the little sanderlings and plovers that darted along the waterline. And no shorebird she had ever seen had a beak like this one. Long and thicker than most, it almost glowed with a brilliant red-orange color, made even brighter by its dark black head and neck. As its search for breakfast brought it warily closer, Lily could see a matching fiery ring around the deep black eye.

Then the strange-looking bird stopped and cocked its head at Lily. She stood as still as she could, her hands clenched together against her chest to hold in any movement that might send the bird flapping away from her. She realized she wasn't breathing. She exhaled a narrow stream of air. The bird's neck feathers ruffled and, for a moment, Lily thought her breath had done it; she felt that close. But she was still a good fifteen feet away.

The bird shook its head to shuffle the misplaced feathers back into place. A quick turn of the neck and the long orange bill darted over and under an outstretched wing. For the first time Lily could see a stark white stripe running along the edge of the deep brown wing.

Its short preening session over, the bird looked again at Lily. "Go ahead," it seemed to say. "Say something about my beak. You humans and your pointy fingers. 'Look, Daddy! Look at that funny bird!' Point, point, point. 'Is that a clown bird?'" But Lily wasn't pointing. She was just looking.

"I'm sorry," she whispered to the bird. She wasn't sure why. It felt halfway like an apology for all her fellow humans and their index fingers and halfway like she was saying, "I know how you feel."

Lily decided she had to know this bird's name. She rushed back up the beach and told her dad she was ready to go.

"But I'm only halfway through the newspaper," he said with surprise. "Usually I have to read the whole thing twice before you wander back."

"I have to do some research," was all she said.

Back at home, feeling wind-blown and gritty, Lily pulled a bright blue book from the shelf in the living room. Between the flamingo and the black-necked stilt she found it: American oystercatcher. The small painting on the page didn't quite convey the true nature of the bill's color, but there was no mistaking it. The name, though, was not what she was expecting. Red-nosed sand poker, maybe, but oystercatcher? She read the description: "Usually seen apart from other shorebirds," the book said.

"I know how you feel," Lily muttered.

She read more. "The bird's long bill is perfectly designed for removal of the meat of oysters and other bivalves." Bivalves? Lily made a mental note to look that one up. "The bill is reinforced to be especially strong and unbending." The name made a little more sense to her, but then she thought for a second about catching oysters. "You don't *catch* oysters," she mumbled to herself. "It's not like they can run away from you." She suddenly pictured an oyster running down the beach yelling, "Help, the birds are after me!" and she laughed out loud. Then she realized she was being like the pointing-finger kids. *"Oystercatcher! What a stupid name!"*

When she went to bed that night she saw glowing red orange behind her closed eyelids.

The next day, she was back on the beach after a short bike ride and a long bus ride. She didn't wander this time, but marched back to the driftwood-and-seaweed spot from yesterday. The quick spish-spish of her shoes slowed as she neared the place where her oystercatcher should have been.

"It's not there," she said into the breeze. Of course it wasn't. It was a wild animal, not a statue. What was she thinking? She turned her head and scanned the edge of the marsh. Nothing.

Then, as a pickup truck full of hopeful fishermen roared along the waterline she heard an unusual rattling call. She turned toward the sound. Her heart jumped as she saw the telltale flash of reddish orange. The truck had startled two of them from behind a ridge of sand just out of Lily's view. Two of them! She had imagined that her oystercatcher was the only one in the world—that the picture in the book had been a personal portrait. But here were two. The realization sent a thrill through Lily. This strange animal, whose ridiculous but beautiful beak stuck out like a sore thumb in this environment—a place that seemed to have a rule against bright colors—was actually perfectly at home here.

Lily realized then, as she watched the two birds settle back to the beach, that she'd been wrong about the look that red-ringed eye had given her yesterday. The oystercatcher didn't care that it didn't look like it belonged on this beach. And it certainly didn't care that it had a silly name like oystercatcher. All the finger-pointing in the world wouldn't change that.

Lily turned to head back north up the beach and toward home. She wanted to stay and watch all day, but there was homework to be done. Monday and school were looming. As she walked, Lily thought again about what her mom had said about the world making no sense: "That's just part of being twelve years old. It's true all over the world. In China, in United States—even for twelve-year-olds on the moon!" Lily imagined a young girl just like her out in space, walking along the sandy lunar surface, wishing she could catch a rocket to somewhere else. Then she stopped and looked back at the birds, now just dark spots moving along the beach. She smiled, happy that this was her home. There weren't any oystercatchers on the moon.

Joe Shepherd *is a Peabody Award–winning radio producer and an avid hiker and bird-watcher. During his ten years in Washington, D.C., he spent as much time as possible escaping to the marshes and beaches of the Chesapeake Bay. He now lives in St. Louis with his wife and two daughters and two dogs. There are no beaches there.*

In the Dune Forest

LYNN SCHUESSLER

The secret creatures of dune and hollow,
Thicket and forest, surround me.
Wolf spiders burrow behind silken doors,
While doodlebugs wait in ambush
At the bottoms of slippery sand traps.
The slithery trail of a hognose snake
Lures me into the brush.
Startled, it hisses and lunges,
Then finally gives up and plays dead.

A box turtle locks itself inside its shell,
Pretending not to be home.
Catbirds and warblers call out unseen,
Playing Marco Polo in the thicket.
Browsers and prowlers, disguised by the night,
Leave clues in their tracks—
Foxes and cottontails, deer and raccoons
Now hide from the bright heat of day.

Lynn Schuessler *learned to love the beach as a child, and has lived on both the East and West Coasts. She now raises a family, writes, and practices physical therapy in York, Pennsylvania.*

Hampton Wetlands

P. G. BRAKE

For many decades, people thought swamps, marshes, and other wetlands were soggy wastelands better drained and filled than protected in their natural state. But now we recognize that wetlands help purify our water and serve as both home and larder for a slew of wild creatures. And, as P. G. Brake describes in this essay, they provide many small pleasures to the people who live in their midst.

I grew up in Hampton, Virginia, which means I grew up with some wonderful wetlands. Fingers of creeks and rivers tickled most parts of the city, and wetlands edged each one. Those wet areas could be cattail stands on the banks of tadpole-filled ditches, like the one we crossed on our walk to school. Or, they could be gradual slopes with musty smelling bayberry bushes and fine, black mud so mucky it actually sucked the boots off my friend Patty's feet one time.

Some wetlands were wide stretches of marsh grasses many feet taller than people. The grasses were so thick the air stood still under them. Only their tops got brushed by the breezes sweeping over the marsh. When the grasses nudged against one another, a quiet whooshing, whiskering sound danced overhead from one side of the marsh to the other.

On a hazy August day, it was drippy and miserable every-place but where our feet were planted in the cool goop. Faces stayed so hot and sweaty that noses were always slippery. My friends who wore eyeglasses had a hard time of it, always jabbing their noses to push their glasses back up. We slapped at bugs a lot, too, to keep from getting bitten. There were more bugs than hands, though, so it didn't work well. Wet, stagnant places bred so many buzzing, blood-hungry bugs that even the slow-moving planes rumbling overhead spraying insecticide didn't get rid of them.

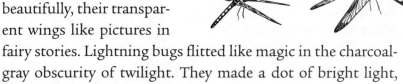

Not all the bugs were annoying. Dragonflies flew beautifully, their transparent wings like pictures in fairy stories. Lightning bugs flitted like magic in the charcoal-gray obscurity of twilight. They made a dot of bright light, then not; here, then there, then up some.

The birds never seemed to mind the weather. Ducks waddled quacking and grumbling into backyards by canals. Geese slept standing on one foot, the other folded up under them. They reached their long necks around so their heads rested

on their backs, tucking their bills slightly under their wings. The bulbous forms of herons blended into both sun glare and grasses until they spread their wings wider than a person is tall and, with a low, slow, floppy flight, moved a few yards over.

One marsh I was especially fond of was in a nature preserve. It eased the transition from the city to the Chesapeake Bay. I went there in the summers on scalding asphalt roads steaming in afternoon thunderstorms. Even my flip-flops couldn't keep the soles of my feet from sweltering on those roads. As soon as I reached a cooler path in moist marsh dirt, I went barefoot just to ease the heat. That path through the tall grasses gradually got grittier until my toes had to grab onto sand in order to walk. The path ended as it rose to a small sand dune. Over the dune's peak came the sizzling beach that made my legs hop while I dropped my flip-flops back on. A few more strides and I was barefoot again, my feet sinking into the soothing wet sand of the intertidal zone.

Growing up in Hampton, Virginia, meant learning that fingers of water tickled more than land. The people who visited and those who resided, the animals that migrated and those that stayed, the plants that grew around the water and those that grew in it: they were all tickled by Hampton's wetlands.

P. G. Brake grew up in Hampton, Virginia, and explored wetlands while attending the Hampton city schools and benefiting from its science enrichment programs. She has a B.A. in environmental science and an M.S. in microbiology.

Heron Bay

MARTIN GALVIN

There is a space for winter here
To grow its ice. There is a place
For a small boat with oars and sail.
There is a piece of water here
For a fish farmer and his old wife,
Turned by the wind into the wind.
We say the night heron stands and waits
For breaking water. He knows that water yields,
That fishes break. His neck is a white slake
Fishing for the water's sake and his.
He takes only his place which is as small
As he needs. He leaves the rest to you
And me, a small boat, winter, and a pair
Of old crabbers leaning into the wind,
Space for oceans to turn in, things that bend.

Martin Galvin *lives in Chevy Chase, Maryland, and has published his poems in* Poetry, Orion, Painted Bride Quarterly, The New Republic, The Atlantic Monthly, The Christian Science Monitor, *and* Best American Poetry 1997. *His first book,* Wild Card, *won the Washington Prize in 1989.*

Welcoming the Waves

MÉLINA MANGAL

In the best of weather and circumstances, beaches offer an ideal place to relax and play. But people aren't drawn to the ocean's edge only when they're happy; they also seek the ocean in times of stress, anger, even grief. The ocean is big enough, it seems, to match the great gusto of life as much as the vast mystery of death.

"Not like that, Chou-chou," Granmé scolded again. "You fold it the long way first, then fold again, ehn?"

I bit my tongue, knowing Granmé wouldn't listen to any of my creative towel-folding ideas. For twenty years, she had worked as a housekeeper at the Dolphin Bay Resort and Hotel. For her, there was only one way to fold towels: the right way (which was of course her way). But Mama wasn't letting Granmé fold anything right now. Granmé was sick.

Her brown skin had faded to a dry walnut color. When I was younger, Granmé had towered over me. And even last year, when Granmé had visited us and seen how much I'd grown, she had still been taller. But now she looked like a child, all propped up with fat pillows on her wooden bed. She didn't sound sick, though. Granmé's strong, sharp voice still cut through the humid air the way it always had.

"More water, Chou-chou," Granmé ordered. *Tro chò*—too hot, ehn?"

I bristled every time Granmé called me by my baby nickname. And she kept repeating everything in English as if I didn't understand Kreyol. I wasn't born in Haiti, like she was. But Mama had been born there, and still spoke Kreyol to me. So I understood it perfectly well, even if I answered back only in English.

I put down the towel, though, happy for a break. I wished Mama had taken me with her when she went to the store. But she said I had to stay with Granmé, "in case she needs something." In case she needs someone to order around, I thought.

I looked out the kitchen window as I filled Granmé's glass with water. A glint of sparkly water from the next-door apartment's pool caught my eye, and a pang of wanting filled me. Why can't I be out at the beach, or even in a pool, swimming like every other fourteen-year-old, I wondered?

I'd felt such excitement when Mama and I had driven across the Intercoastal Highway into Fort Lauderdale the week before. We had come in during rush hour, and Mama had taken the wrong exit off the I-95 freeway. I saw the ocean waving green and blue at me. I had wanted to go swimming right then. But Mama had been driving for eight hours that day. And that was the third day of driving from Minnesota.

When we'd left Saint Paul, Mama had promised me I'd have plenty of time to go to the beach and swim. I had heard Mama tell Dad she was lucky she could take a couple of weeks to help her mother out this summer. But I didn't feel lucky at all. Since we'd arrived, all I'd been doing was sweeping, folding, cleaning, and fetching. It was a lot like being back home with my little brothers. I wanted Granmé to feel better, but this was supposed to be my summer vacation. When would I get a chance to have fun?

"Chou-chou?" Granmé called from her room. Couldn't she wait one minute?

I turned away from the tiny patch of sparkling pool water and headed back to the bedroom. "Why are you so sour-faced, Chou-chou?" Granmé asked as I handed her the glass of water. She drank it up like a thirsty kitten.

"Granmé," I said as nicely as I could muster, "I prefer my real name, Chloe."

Granmé eyed me like a cat would eye a mouse. "Well, as long as I'm livin', you'll always be my little cabbage head, *ti chou-chou*, ehn?"

I sighed and looked at the shaded window. I hated dark rooms. "*Ta mè*—your mama, she pulled the shade down on me. Open the window for me, ehn, Chou-chou?"

I stared out the window at the splash of color beyond. Granmé had a tiny garden. But it had enough color to fill my whole neighborhood back in Saint Paul.

"*Alé déyo*—go outside and get me some flowers. Brighten this place up," Granmé ordered. Mama had bought yellow roses the day after we'd arrived, but they'd faded and wilted into sad crumples.

I felt instantly better when I stepped outside, even though the air was thick with heat. The tall palms beyond the tiny yard swayed in the breeze. Most of them stood straight and tall, like guards. Some leaned over, wanting to tell a secret. Their trunks were propped up by wooden stakes at the bottom, to keep them perfectly straight, I guess. And most of them looked wrapped, as though you could peel off the bark in one long strip, like an Ace bandage. Giant silky green palms sprouted out of the top, like a plume of tail feathers from an exotic bird.

A sweet scent hovered in the air from the honeysuckle bush next to the mailbox. Gnarly gray wisteria vines hung their purple flower clusters from the top of the concrete wall. Sunny orange roses nestled next to the red-veined crotons that seemed to be everywhere. In the corner of the tiny yard were pink azaleas and white camellias.

I saw little flowers poking out of the vines that crawled up the concrete wall. The flowers were a bright magenta. Their petals were shaped like leaves, coming together to form little Chinese paper lanterns with three long green pods inside. One of the pods had opened up and inside, at the end, I could see a tiny yellow star.

I reached out to touch one flower, then saw the thorns—small green ones sticking out along the stem. They were the same color as the stem and the curling leaves. I wanted some flowers anyway, so I carefully pulled some of the stems off the wall. I'd only plucked a few before I heard Granmé's sharp voice calling from inside.

I took the bright blossoms and brushed past the red hibiscus bush, dreading the cool darkness inside the house. "They're not real flowers, Chou-chou," Granmé said when I stepped in the room. "That's bougainvillea—it's a vine. We have them all over Haiti, too. *Ta mè*, she used to like them, just like you do."

I leaned on the dresser, not wanting to sit down. Granmé continued. "And when I was a little girl, whenever we kids would play *kache kache*, the hiding game, I would always hide the rock in a cluster of bougainvillea." Granmé laughed, remembering how the others reacted. "You see, Chou-chou, that's why I always won!" Granmé laughed even harder.

She laughed so hard, I started laughing. When Granmé laughed, her whole face crinkled up and her eyes sparkled like the sun on the water. I realized then that I hadn't heard her laugh since we'd arrived. I preferred Granmé like this, laughing, or at least smiling a little. Why didn't anyone know what was causing her sickness?

"Oh, *sa sifi*—that's enough, Chou-chou," Granmé said after a few minutes. "Go get me some tissues, to wipe my eyes. This box is empty." She held up the empty Kleenex box and shook it.

I obeyed and went into the kitchen. Mama walked in the door moments later. "Help me put these groceries away, Chloe. Then you can go hang out for a while." Mama smiled at me.

I practically threw everything in the refrigerator, then headed out the door. Granmé called my name and said something else as the screen door slammed behind me. I knew Mama would help her, so I kept going. I walked past the red hibiscus again, out the gate, to the corner.

I walked past a hair salon with a whitewashed wall and stopped when something scurried in front of me. It wasn't a bug and it wasn't a bird. It was green and blue and as big as my hand. I watched it slink along the wall the way Spider-Man

would. Could it be one of those skinks
Granmé kept telling me to watch out for?
She'd mentioned them so much the last
time I was here, warning me not to let them in
the house, that I was afraid of seeing one. And I never
did. Until now.

Then I saw a real lizard. Its back looked like a ridged
rock, and it popped its throat out when it breathed. Its throat
and chin turned into an orange-red balloon. I could have
stared at the thing for hours.

Droplets of water began to fall on my back. Within seconds, the sky had opened up. Rain gushed down on me. The
wind bent the palmettos back as it poured and poured.

I wished I'd paid more attention to the sky before I left. It
had rained the day before, too. Would it rain like this every
day?

I ran back, splashing myself with each step. Luckily, the
rain was warm. It felt good! Part of me wanted to stay out and
play in it. But I knew Mama and Granmé would worry. So I
kept running.

When I burst in the back door, Mama met me with a towel
and a smile. "Wet enough for you out there?"

I didn't find it funny. How would she like to be cooped up
all day with Granmé?

"Chou-chou?" Granmé called from her room.

I kicked off my sandals and dripped into her room.
Granmé took one look at me and cracked into laughter again.

"Chou-chou! You look like a soaking seal!"

I shook my head so that my ponytail sent droplets of water
flying.

Granmé shook her head. "I tried to tell you. *Lapli paré*—it looks like it's going to rain. It rains at four o'clock. But you were already running out the door." Granmé laughed even more! Now this was too much. Did Granmé think she could command the weather too?

"No, Chou-chou," Granmé said, winking like she'd read my mind. I froze, waiting for her to continue.

"Come summer, the rains start right on time to cool things off a bit. But don't worry," she continued, nodding to the window. "It should be over by six o'clock."

Mama told Granmé about her medical tests at the hospital in Miami the next day and how we'd have to get up early. It wasn't until later, after Granmé kicked us out of her room so she could nap, that I found out: Granmé was right. The rain stopped right before six. With all that Granmé knew, why didn't she want to know what was wrong with her?

The drive to the hospital the next morning was awful. Mama and Granmé argued the whole way there. They argued about doctors, food, which roads to take, and even how long we should stay. I just stared out the window, catching glimpses of the ocean when I could. I pretended I wasn't there.

We got close enough at one point so that I could see the clear beige sand through the window. I always thought the ocean would look the way the sky does at night—a massive deep blue blanket. But I saw then that it's striped: wavy stripes of light blue, aqua, and steely blue dotted with sailboats and ships. When would I be able to get in?

Mama pulled up in front of the hospital entrance, and we got out of the car. "Chou-chou," Granmé said, "give me your shoulder." She put her arm on me to steady herself. I was surprised at how light it felt. She had always seemed so solid.

We walked past a crowd of smokers into the lobby of the hospital and waited for Mama to park the car. She didn't take long, but everything else did. We shuttled Granmé from one area of the hospital to another. With each move, Granmé grew crankier.

Around three o'clock, Mama told me we had to leave. "Granmé has to stay overnight for the biopsy," she told me. "Let's get some air." Granmé looked happy to see us go. I guessed she was still angry with Mama for bringing her there.

We drove silently toward Coconut Grove, and down to Matheson Hammock Park. I still didn't know what was wrong with Granmé but I'd overheard Mama on the phone with Dad the night before. She mentioned "the C word"—just like that, as if saying the whole word could actually curse Granmé with it. I really hoped Granmé didn't have cancer, though. How could she?

"Thanks for hanging in there with me, and helping Granmé so much," Mama said when we got out of the car. "She appreciates it, too, even though you can't always tell."

I didn't say anything. I'd been wanting to come to the beach, and now here I was, without my swimsuit. I was worried about Granmé, too. "How long will she have to be in the hospital?" I asked.

"She'll be out tomorrow. If all goes well." Mama picked up a stone and tried to skip it across the water. The stone sank without a bounce.

"What do you think's wrong with her?" I asked, dipping my bare feet in the warm water.

Mama took a deep breath and looked at a large, brown pelican flying smooth and low, just above the water. "Chloe, I didn't want you to worry before, but now I think you should know. Granmé is having a biopsy to determine how far her cancer has spread and what can be done to stop it."

My heart sank. Mama had known that Granmé had cancer. I stared at Mama, following her gaze again. The pelican dove straight into the water. It came up with a fish in its long bill. But the fish quickly disappeared down its laundry-hamper-like pouch. When I looked back, tears ran down Mama's face.

"It OK, Mama," I told her. "Granmé is tough. She'll get better." Mama took my hand in hers and we walked into the waves, letting the sea soak our legs. It didn't matter that our shorts were getting wet.

On the horizon, flashes of lightning danced across the darkening sky, like veins of light. A few minutes later, a crash of thunder hit, and the rain started. "Aah!" shrieked Mama before laughing. I started laughing too as she pulled me across the beach toward the car. It was four o'clock. The rain was right on time.

"*Alé la,*" Granmé directed Mama out of the hospital parking lot the next day. "Turn there." I didn't know where we were going, but I knew it wasn't back to Granmé's house. Mama followed each command, biting her lip so she wouldn't say anything. Mama wouldn't say it, but I could tell she was relieved to see Granmé barking orders again.

The beach! Granmé had directed Mama to the beach, a different one from the day before. When Mama stopped the car, we just sat there, waiting for Granmé to say something. She looked at us like we were fools and said, "*Ebyin, ann alé!* Let's go!"

I gave Granmé my shoulder and we walked down to the wet

sand. Granmé didn't want to stop, so I kicked off my sandals and kept walking into the water.

"Manmi, you're getting yourself all wet!" Mama shouted to Granmé.

"*Ebyin,* of course I am!" Granmé shouted back. She waved at Mama to come join us, and Mama did. We held Granmé in between us and watched her as she welcomed the waves. She smiled each time the water splashed against her shins and lapped up the beach.

"Oh, *sa sifi*—that's enough, Chou-chou," Granmé said after a while. She turned to Mama and squeezed her cheek as if she were a little baby. Mama hugged her, and wouldn't let go.

Granmé eyed me behind Mama and said, "*Alé*—Go on. Jump in like you've been wanting to."

I stepped away, farther into the water to give them peace. Once again, I was at the beach without my bathing suit. I looked at Mama and Granmé again. This time, Granmé gave me a wink.

That choked me up. So I dove into the next wave, no longer caring how I might look swimming in my shorts and T-shirt. I splashed and swam and dove into each new wave, not wanting to look back at Granmé and Mama.

I don't know how long I kept that up, but when I did look, they were sitting in the sand. I waded back in and plopped down next to them. Granmé was smiling.

"Here," she said, handing me a shell, "I found something special for you." It looked like a large snail shell, swirled with spikes. But its underside had bright pink flecks. It was beautiful.

"We walked all the way to that hotel and back," Mama said, pointing with pride.

"Thanks, Granmé," I said. "*Mesi.*"

"No matter how far away you are," Granmé said, smiling and wiggling her toes in the sand, "you'll always have a piece of the sea with you."

And I'll always have a piece of you with me, too, Granmé, I wanted to say. But I just sat down, laughing with her and Mama as we welcomed the tide.

Mélina Mangal *is a librarian and children's writer living in Saint Paul, Minnesota.*

Coming of Age
in the Tropics

GRETCHEN FLETCHER

How's a teenage girl to feel
when the sticky, thick scents
of gardenias, frangipani,
and night-blooming jasmine

come through her bedroom window,
and the night's so hot
it makes her sheets wet
so she takes her pillow outside

and sleeps on the prickly zoysia-
grass blades under the palm tree
where the fronds filter moonlight
into stripes on her face?

How's a teenage girl to feel
as she squashes the ripe red flesh
of fallen Surinam cherries
with bare, tanned feet

or when she halves a fallen avocado
and squirts onto its velvety yellow meat

the tangy juice of a Key lime
she found in the white sand?

How's she to feel
when she breaks star-shaped flowers
from the ixora hedge and sucks
drops of nectar from their long stems?

How's she to feel
when everything's blooming or in bud
and her backyard's full
of alamandas, oleander,

bougainvillea and hibiscus,
with only ficus and banyan trees
to shade her from the heat,
and the names of the other trees,

Australian pines and Brazilian pepper,
sound like places to run away to?
How's a teenage girl to feel
coming of age in the tropics?

Gretchen Fletcher's personal essays, travel articles, and poetry
appear frequently in newspapers, literary journals, and anthologies.
She leads writing workshops for the Florida Center for the Book and
teaches fifth grade at a private school in Fort Lauderdale.

Longleaf

JANISSE RAY

Janisse Ray grew up in a junkyard in rural Georgia. As a child, she spent long stretches of time in the outdoors. But only as an adult did she become familiar with the native habitats of her homeland—most notably, the grand forests of longleaf pine that once grew in spectacular abundance across the state.

My homeland is about as ugly as a place gets. There's nothing in south Georgia, people will tell you, except straight, lonely roads, one-horse towns, sprawling farms, and tracts of planted pines. It's flat, monotonous, used-up, hotter than hell in summer, and cold enough in winter that orange trees won't grow. No mountains, no canyons, no rocky streams, no waterfalls. The rivers are muddy, wide and flat, like somebody's feet. The coastal plain lacks the stark grace of the desert or the umber panache of the pampas. Unless you look close, there's little majesty.

It wasn't always this way. Even now in places, in the Red Hills near Thomasville, for example, and on Fort Stewart Military Reservation near Hinesville, you can see how south Georgia used to be, before all the old longleaf pine forests that were our sublimity and our majesty were cut. Nothing is more beautiful, nothing more mysterious, nothing more breathtaking, nothing more surreal.

Longleaf pine is the tree that grows in the upland flat-woods of the coastal plains. Miles and miles of longleaf and wiregrass, the ground cover that coevolved with the pine, once covered the left hip of North America—from Virginia to the Florida peninsula, west past the Mississippi River: longleaf as far in any direction as you could see. In a longleaf forest, miles of trees forever fade into a brilliant salmon sunset and re-appear the next dawn as a battalion marching out of fog. The tip of each needle carries a single drop of silver. The trees are so well spaced that their limbs seldom touch and sunlight streams between and within them. Below their flattened branches, grasses arch their tall, richly dun heads of seeds, and orchids and lilies paint the ground orange and scarlet. Purple liatris gestures across the landscape. Our eyes seek the flowers like they seek the flashes of birds and the careful crossings of forest animals. . . .

What thrills me most about longleaf forests is how the pine trees sing. The horizontal limbs of flattened crowns hold the wind as if they are vessels, singing bowls, and air stirs in them like a whistling kettle. I lie in thick grasses covered with sun and listen to the music made there. This music cannot be heard anywhere else on the earth.

Rustle, whisper, shiver, whinny. Aria, chorus, ballad, chant. Lullaby. In the choirs of the original groves, the music must have resounded for hundreds of miles in a single note of rise and fall, lift and wane, and stirred the red-cockaded

woodpeckers nest-
ing in the hearts of
these pines, where I
also nest, child of soft
heart. Now we strain to
hear the music; anachronous,
it has an edge. It falters, a great
tongue chopped in pieces.

Something happens to you in an old-
growth forest. At first you are curious to see
the tremendous girth and height of the trees,
and you sally forth, eager. You start to saunter,
then amble, slower and slower, first like a fox and
then an armadillo and then a tortoise, until you are
trudging at the pace of an earthworm, and then even
slower, the pace of a sassafras leaf's turning. The blood be-
gins to languish in your veins, until you think it has turned
to sap. You hanker to touch the trees and embrace them and
lean your face against their bark, and you do. You smell them.
You look up at leaves so high their shapes are beyond focus,
into far branches with circumferences as thick as most trees.

Every limb of your body becomes weighted, and you have
to prop yourself up. There's this strange current of energy
running skyward, like a thousand tiny bells tied to your capil-
laries, ringing with your heartbeat. You sit and lean against
one trunk—it's like leaning against a house or a mountain.
The trunk is your spine, the nerve centers reaching into other
worlds, below ground and above. You stand and press your
body into the ancestral and enduring, arms wide, and your fingers do not touch. You wonder how big the unseen gap.

If you stay in one place too long, you know you'll root.

I drink old-growth forest in like water. This is the homeland that built us. Here I walk shoulder to shoulder with history—my history. I am in the presence of something ancient and venerable, perhaps of time itself, its unhurried passing marked by immensity and stolidity, each year purged by fire, cinched by a ring. Here mortality's roving hands grapple with air. I can see my place as human in a natural order more grand, whole, and functional than I've ever witnessed, and I am humbled, not frightened, by it. Comforted. It is as if a round table springs up in the cathedral of pines and God graciously pulls out a chair for me, and I no longer have to worry about what happens to souls.

After living away from the region for many years, **Janisse Ray** *has returned to rural Georgia, where she lives on a farm with her son. This excerpt comes from her memoir,* Ecology of a Cracker Childhood.

Ponte Vedra Beach

MARIANNE POLOSKEY

For my aunt, Hilde

We spent years of afternoons
at the beach, lounging
on sand-padded blankets
in the spotlight of the sun
that slowly walked around us
never letting us out of sight,
as if we were children
to be looked after

while the wind,
tearing at our hair,
swept the shore
with the flapping sound
of billowing sails.

We talked or just watched
the waves roar in,
white-fringed crowns
that hesitated at the top,
hunched into huge transparent seashells
that pounced forward—
and finally the tumble,
the running away.

As the air began to cool
we shook the afternoon
from our blanket and rolled it up
around the ocean's smell.

On the way back, you always
drove fast, as if leaving
the scene of a loss
or to catch up with reality.
By the time we reached town,
day had closed its doors—
but the cries of gulls
followed us all the way home.

Marianne Poloskey *lived in Florida for about five years. She has contributed poetry to many publications, including* The Christian Science Monitor, North American Review, Palo Alto Review, Paterson Literary Review, *and* Louisiana Literature. *Her first book of poems was* Climbing the Shadows.

Paynes Prairie

ARCHIE CARR

Central Florida is home to a unique habitat called wet prairie. Wet prairies are neither as wet as a marsh nor as dry as a dry prairie. Instead they offer a middle ground, a submerged, moist kingdom filled with large numbers of reptiles and amphibians, and many other fascinating sights.

Paynes Prairie is fifty square miles of level plain in north-central Florida let down in the hammock and pinelands south of Gainesville by collapse of the limestone bedrock. It drains partly into Orange Lake to the south and partly into a sinkhole at its northeast side. The sink used to clog up occasionally, and for years or decades the prairie would be under water. The people called it Alachua Lake in those times and ran steamboats on it.

Nowadays the prairie is mostly dry, with shallow ponds and patches of marsh where ancient gator holes have silted up but never disappeared, and with patches of Brahma cattle here and there out into the far spread of the plain, like antelope in Kenya. The prairie is about the best thing to see on U.S. Route 441 from the Smoky Mountains to the Keys, though to tell why would be to digress badly. But everybody with any sense is crazy about the prairie. The cowboys who work there like it and tell with zest of unlikely creatures they see—a black panther was the last I heard of—and people fish for bowfins in the ditches. There used to be a great vogue in snake catching on the prairie before the roadsides became a sanctuary. People from all around used to come and catch the snakes that sunned themselves along the road shoulders. When William Bartram was there the prairie wrought him up, and his prose about the place was borrowed by Coleridge for his poem "Kubla Khan." The prairie has changed since then, with all the wolves and the Indians gone. But still there are things to make a crossing worth your while, to make it, as I said, the best two miles in all the long road south from the mountains.

I live on one side of the prairie and work on the other side. I have crossed a thousand times. Two thousand times. And always it is something more than getting to work or going home. I have seen the cranes dance there, and a swallowtail kite, and, on the road during one crossing, 765 snakes. And there was an early morning in October that I remember. It was after a gossamer day, a day when the spiders had been flying, young spiders and old of a number of kinds, ballooning to new places in the slow flood of a southeast wind. Some of them traveled no more than ten paces, riding the pull of their hair-thin threads for the space between two bushes. Some went by a thousand feet up, streaming off to Spain on jagged white ribbons like thirty feet of spun sugar against the sky. By nightfall the whole plain was covered with the silk of their landings. As far as you could see, the prairie was spread with a thin tissue of the dashed hopes and small triumphs of spiders, held up by the grass tips, draped over every buttonbush and willow.

We drove by in the early mist-hindered morning. The dew was down, and the drops formed strands of beads in acres of silken webbing. The fog had flaws in it here and there, and the sun coming through turned the plain all aglow, like a field of opals, and I slowed the car to look. Up toward the east from the road a Brahma bull stood in the edge of the sea of silk, and as I stopped on the shoulder across from where he was he raised his head to look our way. He was stern and high-horned and stood straight up from the forequarters, like an all-bull centaur. Suddenly the sunlight touched him, and my wife and I fell to beating at each other, each to be first to say: "Look at his horns." The bull had gone grazing in the night, and now his horns were all cross-laced with silk picked up from the grass. He stood there with the sun rising behind him, and his horns were like a tall lyre strung with strings of seed pearls gathered in the mist and burning in the slanted light.

There is no telling the things you see on the prairie. To a taste not too dependent upon towns, there is always something, if only a new set of shades in the grass and sky or a round-tail muskrat bouncing across the blacktop or a string of teal running low with the clouds in the twilight in front of the winter wind. The prairie is a solid thing to hold to in a world all broken out with man. There is peace out there, and quiet to hear rails calls and cranes bugling in the sky.

Born in Mobile, Alabama, **Archie Carr** *spent most of his life in Florida, where he taught biology at the University of Florida. He was the author of many books, and a leading researcher on sea turtles.*

Lessons of the Road: Crossing the Florida-Georgia State Line

LARRY RUBIN

To wake up on the other side, not realizing,
At first, only vaguely aware that something
Has slightly altered. Maybe the diminished
Clumps of scrub palmetto—not gone,
But smaller, fewer, less intense, looking
Fearful of subtraction. The pines are clearly
Dominant, tinkling in their turpentine cups,
Below their stripped-off bark, though oaks
Crop up, some even yellow-tinged
In early fall. The sky itself delivers
Hints, its blue more powder than azure.
And now the landscape rolls, a miracle
Of geology. You sense the loss of al-
Ligators, the sudden possibility—
A little further on—of latitude's lofty
Game: The pointed code, the prize, of snow.

Larry Rubin *is the author of several collections of poetry. He lives in Atlanta, Georgia.*

A February Walk in Georgia

MARY ANN COLEMAN

On a winter day
I walked a wooded path
the décor all browns and grays.
Even the starlings in the tops of trees
posed like weather-blackened leaves.

Still
in time
I began to see—
the heraldry of shadows
on the ground; branches of bare oaks,
rich mosses fit for the thrones of kings,
the sun's bronze medal warming the cold sky.
Walking deeper still, I found a quince
sending forth its greeting of tight red buds,
a fern unrolling its delicate lace surprise
and by a creek, a weeping willow
standing in its own green rain.

Then, I began to hear—
the heavy silences of plants
pushing earth aside,
the silken rustle of pine needles:

small brooms brushing the air—
making way for April.
The rising-falling call of tree frogs
and overhead, the beating
of the wings
of one lone hawk
circling.

A woods
dreaming its way
toward spring.

Mary Ann Coleman's *poems have appeared in anthologies, text-books, and journals such as* Spider, Cricket, Kansas Quarterly, *and* International Quarterly. *Her own books include* The Dreams of Hummingbirds, *a collection of nature poetry for children. She lives in Athens, Georgia.*

Reapers and Sowers

My Country Garden

FELICIA MITCHELL

The dog fennel transplanted
from the fields of Toogoodoo
to our backyard in town
snapped in my fingers
like beans in my mother's
as I inhaled the odor
that made my brother sneeze.

And the rabbit tobacco
made it to harvest,
offering a more pungent taste
than the honeysuckle blossoms
we sucked from the fence
or the vinegar and honey
my mother mixed to ward off colds.

Only the sound of quail
was missing from my garden
tucked between an apple tree
and our neighbor's boxwoods.
I remember making bird calls, though,
and hammering a fence of wood scraps
to keep the lawn mower out.

Felicia Mitchell *grew up in North Carolina and South Carolina. She now resides in Virginia, where she teaches at Emory & Henry College, but maintains close ties with South Carolina. Her poems have appeared in a variety of journals and a chapbook, and her most recent scholarly project involved editing* Her Words: Diverse Voices in Contemporary Appalachian Women's Poetry *(University of Tennessee Press).*

Catch of the Day

Michael W. Raymond

In the lakes and ponds of Florida, a wild assortment of fish and reptiles lurks beneath the surface, adding to the thrill and unpredictability of any fishing trip.

The two bicycles clanked across the bridge, stopping just between the canal and the cattle guard. Bruce jumped off his bike and walked it across the rattly metal bars. He unlocked and opened the gate. Al wheeled both bikes through the gate and waited for his brother to close and lock it.

"Let's go. The bass are waiting."

The bikes fishtailed down the sandy dirt road through the orange grove. The rows and rows of recently picked trees waved up and down the rolling hills of Lake County. They were squat and green and looked like soldiers at ease. Al turned left around the fruit pickers' shed and pedaled to another fence. The gate through the inner fence didn't have a lock.

The brothers eased down the slope. For the last two hundred feet down the road, they flew through a section of creeping kudzu, untamed brush, and new pine trees. Then they burst into a clearing with a mid-sized grove pond. Al and Bruce sized up their favorite fishing hole. The afternoon Florida downpours had done wonders for the pond. The water was high. It looked about five hundred yards long and a hundred yards across. A faint breeze curled down from the stand of huge water oaks at the north end, rippling the blue-green surface of the pond. Only one strand of the barbed wire fence below the oaks could be seen. Lily pads had grown out more than thirty-five feet all along the eastern shoreline. At the south end, a few lily pads, some sawgrass, and then stalks and stalks of bulrushes looked like a green stepladder into the thick Florida landscape. The scrub made the rural landscape seem dark and dangerous.

"Will you look at all that cover," Bruce exclaimed. "The lunker bass must be building retirement homes in there."

Al grunted and turned to their canoe, which was locked to a pine tree. Bruce felt like a Seminole as they held the canoe above their heads to carry it to the water.

"One—two—three—down!"

The slight waves slapped against the canoe as Bruce locked their bikes to the same pine and Al carried their tackle to the pond. Both were silent as they anticipated a great day of fishing. Neither wanted to jinx the spell or let the fish know they were coming. Bruce held the canoe as his older brother gingerly stepped over the rods, reels, and boxes to the back. Once seated, Al signaled Bruce to give them a shove and to hop in. They paddled smoothly to the north end of the pond without a word. Then they dropped two anchors to hold the canoe steady about ten yards from the vegetation and the barbed wire fence.

"What are you going to try?" whispered Bruce.

"A six-inch purple worm, Carolina rigged, no sinker."

"I guess I'll try a green worm with a one-quarter sinker," said Bruce.

After a few casts with their spinning reels, the brothers began to hit the edge of the lily pads, sawgrass, and vegetation nearly every time. They dragged the plastic worms until they dropped off the edge and sank in the three to four feet of dark water. They worked up the fence. Casting, waiting, dragging, dropping, and waiting.

"I know they're in there," hissed Al.

Al changed to a black worm, but Bruce stuck with his lucky green. At the middle of the fence, Bruce felt a nibble. A slight tap-tap-tap on his line. He tried to wait. The line jerked right, and the twelve-year-old set the hook. He'd missed.

"Darn. I was too eager."

"Patience, little brother. These bass didn't get old and fat by being dumb. Let 'em run with it."

Al plopped his black worm on top of a lily pad. Just as he dragged it off the edge, something snatched it and dove. In about three seconds, Al pulled his rod back over his shoulder to set the hook.

"Got you!"

A middle-sized bass came out of the water as if walking on its tail.

"Need some help?"

"No way. This baby's mine. He's not that big anyway."

The bass jumped two more times before it tired. Al drew the fish to the canoe, pressed his thumb down on the big mouth, and lifted it so Bruce could see.

"Not bad, big brother. Maybe two pounds. Let's go get his daddy and granddaddy."

Al unhooked the fish, lowered it into the water, and waited

until it moved before releasing it. As Al was rigging another black plastic worm, Bruce's rod bent nearly double.

"I got a hit!"

"Don't horse it. Let 'em run before you set the hook."

The drag on Bruce's spinning reel whined as the line rolled off. Bruce reared back to set the hook. The line kept going.

"Al, I think this is a big one."

"Work him . . . Let him wear himself out . . . You've got him . . . Don't get impatient." Al put his rod down and made sure the tackle wasn't in Bruce's way.

"This is a big fish, or I've got his side hooked."

"We'll see. Just be ready. He should be coming up, trying to shake your hook when he gets in the air. Keep the line taut."

The fish did not come up. For nearly ten minutes, it stayed on the bottom and tried to get into the thick vegetation. Bruce held the rod high and cranked up line whenever he could.

"Who's going to tire out first—you or the fish?" joked Al.

"He's mine!" exclaimed Bruce. "He's coming up. This is a big one!"

The excited boy began reeling in his prize. The green worm appeared first. It had been knocked up the line about three feet. Bruce reached down to grab the fish as Al had earlier. Just as his hand got near the water, a big splash erupted beside the canoe. Bruce instinctively jerked back.

"Holy cow!" yelled Al.

A wide-open alligator mouth gaped at Bruce. The startled boy could have counted the alligator's teeth. The mouth snapped shut and splashed back into the water. The tail swiped sideways, barely missing the canoe. Both brothers were sprayed with pond water. The alligator took off.

"Break the line, break the line!"

Bruce cut the line with his Swiss army knife. He and Al sat stunned in their canoe on the pond. A few minutes later, the older brother stirred.

"Let's try the other end."

"Suits me," murmured Bruce.

After putting their rods between them, they paddled across the pond.

"How big do you think it was, Al?"

"Oh, about your size—four or four and a half feet."

"I'm bigger than that!"

"Just kidding. We sure were lucky. He could've had your arm for a snack, knocked over the canoe, and had the two of us for dinner."

"That's not funny."

"It wasn't meant to be. We need to keep our eyes open. That may not be the only gator in this pond."

At the south end, the pond was almost like a mirror. The thick hammock of Florida scrub, oaks, and pines kept even the light breeze from disturbing the water's surface. No alligators were in sight. Al removed his fly rod from its case.

"I'm gonna give this a try while the wind's down," he explained. "There's a little pollen on the pond, and the bass might find a sinking bug too much to resist."

"Okay by me," Bruce said. "Just as long as you don't hook me with that flying thing. And don't capsize this canoe. Our newest friend might be out there waiting for us."

They put the canoe east and west on the pond so Al could fly-fish and Bruce could work plastic worms without getting in each other's way. Occasionally Bruce would paddle a stroke or two to move them into a new area.

"Oh boy!"

"What is it, Al?"

"A nice one just picked up my bug. It just rolled and sucked it in. You might want to grab a paddle."

Al's fly rod curled like a question mark at the top. The small fly rod reel whirled as the line peeled off. Whatever Al had hooked took off for about fifteen yards and veered into the lily pads.

"Give me a hand."

Bruce paddled on the outside of the canoe, away from the fish and the pads. The pull of the line kept the nose of the canoe pointed into the vegetation.

"Do you think it's our friend Mr. Alligator?"

"I hope not." Al shook his head. "I don't think so. This one moves pretty fast, and it hardly made a splash when it rolled into the bait."

"Want me to take you into the pads?"

"Yes, let's do it."

Once in the islands of flat, green pads, Al worked hard trying to keep his leader and line free from the lilies or their stems. He looked like an orchestra conductor waving his fly rod wand up, down, and around. Bruce made sure the canoe was almost right above the taut line.

"He's sure stubborn," Al grunted.

Several minutes later, Al's prey changed strategy. It headed out of the pads. The canoe followed. The reel whined once the fighting specimen hit the open water.

"You've got 'em now!" exclaimed Bruce.

The line went slack. Al cranked and cranked.

"He's coming up! This isn't any alligator."

A huge bass broke the water. A massive head opened into a gigantic mouth with winglike gills flapping as the fish waggled its head. The tail just cleared the surface as the arching bass splashed down into the pond. Bruce had seen the yellow bug lodged in the massive jaw. Fear and wonder crossed Al's face as he desperately tried to reel in the excess line.

"I wish we had a net," Bruce muttered.

"I don't want to lose this one, I can't lose this one," mumbled Al.

The bass shot up out of the pond three more times, each time wildly shaking its head and splashing back down into the water. It would run a little and then gain strength for another leap.

"He's going to shake that hook."

"No way, Al, you set it right into his jaw."

Ten minutes passed before Al admitted he might land the biggest fish of his young life. The bass hadn't jumped again, and the fight against the line had weakened. He wasn't satisfied to keep the line taut; he slowly reeled in more and more line. But he remained alert, holding the rod tip high. He braced himself and waited for an unexpected last-ditch effort by the massive beast to escape.

"Are you sure it's not a gator?" teased Bruce.

"You saw . . . ," Al began, then laughed at himself for falling for his brother's joke. "Nah, you're the alligator hunter in this family."

The big bass finally came to the surface. It lolled along the side of the green canoe. Its tail barely waved to keep water going through its gills. The bass and Al were exhausted. Al raised the rod to lift up the fish's jaw. He grunted at the weight of the bass. He showed the trophy to Bruce.

"What do you think? Twelve, thirteen pounds?"

"At least. You are the bass master of Luke's Pond!" Bruce yelled.

"What should we do?"

Bruce frowned. "What do you mean? What should we do? That's a trophy fish. That's a fisherman's dream. You get it mounted, and make the rest of the world kneel at your feet."

"I don't know." Al looked at the bass and then to Bruce. "She sure is big, but she's full of roe. She's just beautiful. And you know what we always say, 'Catch and release. Fish another day.'"

"Are you nuts? Big brother, you may never again catch another fish like this."

"Not if we take her, that's for sure. She could keep this pond stocked for years."

"But Al. She's such a beauty."

"I wish I had a camera," Al said sadly.

Al took one last long look at the catch of the day. Then he used his pliers to remove the fly and hook from the massive jaw. With both hands, he lowered the beautiful bass into the pond water. He frowned. The fish didn't move. He gently pushed and pulled her by the tail along the canoe.

"Come on, baby, you can do it. Come on."

As if in reply, the bass moved its tail. Then she shook her head. Al pushed and pulled her more vigorously. She came to life. He released her. She thrashed away.

At first, Bruce and Al sat in solemn silence. Then grins creased their faces at almost the same time. Finally, they burst into laughter.

"A bad day of fishing is better than a great day at work—or school," Bruce said.

"Where would I have gotten the cash to have that whale stuffed? I'd be in debt for the rest of my life."

"Can you imagine the pressure? Everyone who saw that monster on your wall would want to know where it jumped into our canoe."

"How could we have gotten her home? I'd have to rent a truck. And I don't even have a driver's license."

"Good move, Al."

"Thanks."

The brothers picked up their rods and worked their plastic worms and flies up and down the eastern shore. They contentedly cast and recast their lures into the vegetation as the Florida sun sank behind them on the pond.

Michael W. Raymond *teaches English at Stetson University. He has published three nonfiction books and many essays and stories in journals.*

Shrimping

AMELIA SIDES

Laughter on the water, at the dock, cast and pull,
music of water and voices.
Salt water in the mouth, taste the river mud.
Reach for the net, arm goes down, hold with your teeth, cast,
    spin,
and release.
Breathe.
Crash of water. Spray on the wind.

Hand over hand, cast and pull,
laughter at a caught fish, a squid. Stop to watch a heron.
Missed throw, the net twists.
Crash, pull it in, and throw again.
Laughter as a ten-year-old boy tries to throw a fifty-pound net.
Catch him before he goes in.

Sun goes down in the marsh. Light the lamps.
Cricket sings and moonlight reflects off the water.
Moths hum and bump at the lights, shrimp till the tide changes.

Orange fades to blue, night sky. Night on the marsh, the river.
Sit and watch the tide.

Birds cry, marsh smell of salt and water, marsh mud and
   wood smoke.
Pine bugs whir and scream in the dark. Lap of water on the
   dock.
Tired voices murmur, soft laughter.
A cool breeze whips wet and tired faces.
Cools the body and the mind.

Pack up the nets; blow out the lamps, head home.
Sit in the kitchen and clean shrimp.
Get kicked out of the kitchen and sit on the porch and
   clean shrimp.
Pick up by the antenna, pinch off the head.

Old men drinking beer and telling stories.
Flash of cigarettes in the dark, sweet smoke.
Glow of charcoal, hamburgers on the grill.
Old women in the kitchen cracking jokes, laughter as they cook.
Crabs on the stove, coleslaw on the counter, peanuts on the
   boil.
Life, the river.

A native of Augusta, Georgia, **Amelia Sides** *wrote this poem when
she was eighteen years old and a student at A. R. Johnson High School.
It was a finalist in the 2000 River of Words Poetry and Art Contest.*

Bounty

Paul Jahnige

The first people to live in the area that is now Baltimore were undoubtedly collectors, gathering berries from bushes, fish from streams, and nuts from trees. And although a major city has sprung up on this site over the last several hundred years, the urge to collect lives on.

The summer we came to Baltimore, we lived in a white clapboard house on the edge of Leakin Park. It was an old house, in need of repair, that belonged to the Park Department. The porch slanted noticeably and every time I sat on the upstairs toilet, it sank a little more into the floor, till I was convinced that one day it (and I) would end up on top of the downstairs toilet. But it was a calming place to live in the middle of a city, with acres of woods and miles of trails right out the back door. One morning I even spotted a fox sauntering past our garden plot.

That summer I got to know some of the usual parts of Baltimore. I visited the Inner Harbor to eat dinner from the pavilions overlooking the water. I saw the Orioles win at Camden Yards. I walked along the piers at Fells Point. But I also got to know parts of town that most visitors never see, narrow "inner-block" streets with row houses that are only eleven feet wide, vacant lots struggling to become community gardens, neighborhoods of boarded-up buildings hoping to turn themselves around. It was all part of my job.

You see, I am an urban community forester. I encourage neighborhood residents to plant trees and gardens. I try to convince folks that there is an environment and a forest even in the middle of a city. I seek out the green that makes up that forest, and the greeners who tend it.

As such, I have trained my eyes to see both the community and the forest wherever they grow, sometimes in the least likely spots. That's how I began to understand that not all food comes from a farm, that not all medicines come from a factory, that not all gifts come from a store. The natural world around us, even in a city like Baltimore, can provide such things. We only have to know where to find the bounty of the urban forest, and understand how to collect it with respect.

I first realized it at the Saturday farmer's market at Greenmount Avenue and Thirty-second Street. Earlier in my life I had been to some far-flung places around the world—to the rain forest of Ecuador, to the hills of Sulawesi, even to the upper Congo River. I knew that in these places, people still lived by collecting from the forest. I knew they gathered palm fronds for roofs, monkeys for food, rare barks for medicines, and bamboo for weapons. But I knew we had no forests like those in the eastern United States.

And yet on a fall Saturday at the farmer's market, I noticed a new vendor with a shingle that read Woodland Mushrooms. I asked him where his mushrooms came from. Already he had attracted quite a crowd with his grilled mushroom pita pockets and he was racing around grilling, taking orders, making change, grilling, filling bags with different colored fungi, and did I mention grilling? But between all that I gleaned that many of the different varieties of mushrooms on the table came from the woods behind his home, a home in central Baltimore, on the edge of Druid Hill Park. These were urban mushrooms, collected from the urban forest. His stall was hopping.

A few weeks later, on a wet October morning, I saw two men collecting Chinese chestnuts from a stand of trees along Windsor Mill Road. They were brothers, and they explained in heavy Italian accents that it was too wet to pour concrete, their usual job. Since the nuts were in season, they welcomed the chance to collect some. "My children love them," one told me, "even more than candy. And it's hard to get fresh ones in the store." Remembering the mushroom man, I asked if they ever collected anything else. They immediately invited me into their car and drove just a short distance to where shelves of white fungus were growing on a large log. "In Italian, we call this a shell mushroom—I don't remember what it's called in English. I will take some home for my wife to use in her pasta sauce. It will be a special dinner." I learned later that they were oyster mushrooms, a variety that sells for six dollars a pound at the market. We had picked several pounds of them that afternoon.

I began to get curious about these foods from the urban forest, nontimber forest products, we used to call them in Ecuador. I began asking people I knew if they ever collected. My friend Ms. Lucille, an elderly African American community leader, at first laughed at the idea. But as she thought back to her younger days, she remembered that she and her grand-mother used to collect the long pods of honey locust trees and use them to make some form of home brew. Then she remembered pokeweed or poke sallet. "People still collect it," she said. "It grows everywhere. Don't you know it? Pokeberry—we called it pokeberry too. It's a green. You boil the young leaves for a long time and make it like collards. My grandmother used to make us eat it often to clean out the system." Then she laughed again. "She used to collect ailanthus leaves too." Ailanthus? I thought with surprise. That's the ugliest, weediest, most invasive tree in the city. It's so hardy it grows on every vacant lot and even out of vacant buildings. "What did she do with ailanthus?" I asked. "She boiled it, mixed it with cornmeal and made a healing salve with it, though I don't know how well it worked."

Listening to Ms. Lucille really got me going, and I began seeing collectors everywhere. Ms. Lucille introduced me to Mr. Stout (or Mr. Shorty, as she called him), who tended a beautiful garden on a corner vacant lot only about a block and a half on the "wrong side" of Johns Hopkins Hospital in a neighborhood known as Middle East. His garden had two large pear trees, and during the summer months they were dripping with big beautiful ripe pears. Mr. Stout told me he never had to worry about spraying. There weren't many pests that attacked trees in the middle of the inner city. He had to worry only about hungry passersby, but he guessed those were pears well lost. The best pears always made it inside to his wife. She made pies, preserves, and canned pears that were famous, at least in Middle East. She always shared them with friends and neighbors on the block. Thanks to Mr. Shorty, his wife, and some urban pears, the whole neighborhood had become closer.

As I drove around town, I was constantly on the lookout for people in parks or on roadsides who were stooping, picking or cutting plants, or carrying bags or baskets. One day I noticed two women crouched beside a channelized stream that ran behind a high school. Pulling over, I approached them for a

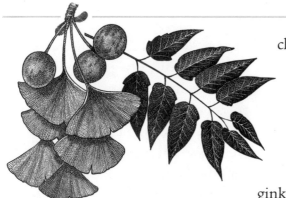

closer look. Both women were elderly Koreans who spoke very little English. But through signing and pointing, they explained that they'd just collected ginkgo fruit from a nearby tree and were washing the smelly pulp from the inside kernel. After a bit of research, I discovered that the ginkgo kernel contains a nut that is highly prized in many kinds of Asian cooking but difficult to find in American stores.

In the spring, while walking through one of Baltimore's steeply pitched stream valley parks, I encountered a Native American gentleman collecting driftwood along a stream. By this time, I'd learned how to start a conversation that usually succeeded in making strangers comfortable enough to share their collecting secrets with me. I came across, I hoped, as a friendly guy with an oddly persistent interest in natural collecting. This gentleman wove for me a story about wood and water and sun and art. He told me how he, as an artist, sought out those special pieces of wood sculpted by the spirits, and molded them further to create works that formed a bridge between the human and spirit worlds. He made dream-catchers, headdresses, and instruments. That day he held a piece of birch. He showed me where the spirits had shaped it. He saw a fine jewelry box in that wood, he said, and he already knew for whom it had been intended. He would mold, stitch, and decorate further, until his gift became the thing that would give his friend strength.

One Sunday afternoon in June, I spotted a man on a

sidewalk, surrounded by a horde of neighborhood kids. As the children held his large umbrella upside down, he shook the branches of a large mulberry tree. Round and round they went, shaking and laughing. Once all the ripe berries had fallen, they trooped inside a nearby house, washed them, and gobbled up all they'd collected.

In July, I took my own daughters out in the buggy for a ride on a hiker-biker trail that stretches like a thread from the northwest quadrant of Baltimore all the way to the inner harbor. On our ride we discovered large patches of wineberry bushes (an invasive, fuzzy, and equally delicious relative of raspberry). An hour later, we headed home with only a pittance in our pails, but a bounty in our bellies, singing our own version of a song from one of the girls' favorite books:

Shrub berry, vine berry, pick me a wineberry,
Yours berry, mine berry, they're so fine berry,
Ridin' on the trail on the Fourth of July,
Picking wineberries for wineberry pie.

The more I look, the more I see. I've met hundreds of urban collectors, and have become one myself. For food, fun, friends, family, even fortune (thought not much of that), people collect from the forests of Baltimore and other cities, too—New York, Chicago, Los Angeles. I think the historians and anthropologists have it wrong when they say we have evolved from hunter-gatherers to farmers and ranchers and grocery store shoppers. Those who have a relationship to the natural world around them will always be hunters and gatherers. There is bounty in the forest wherever we live.

Paul Jahnige *now lives in Williamsburg, Massachusetts, where he works as a community forester for the state and grows mushrooms, garden vegetables, and orchard berries around his home.*

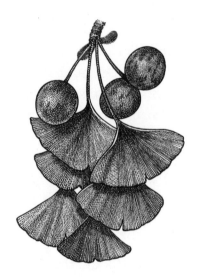

A Haiku and Two Tanka

Lenard D. Moore

Haiku

Family reunion—
    smoke from the grilling steak
        drifts on noonday heat

Tanka

month of rain ends—
hoeing tomatoes for my father
this breezeless day
my cousin waves from rank weeds
and an ambulance passes

Tanka

after church meeting
grandma dumps cornbread batter
in the shiny pan—
the smell of collard greens
lingering on summer air

Lenard D. Moore *was born in Jacksonville, North Carolina. He is the author of* Desert Storm: A Brief History *and* Forever Home. *Twice nominated for the Pushcart Prize, he has written poems, essays, and reviews for more than 350 publications. He teaches English, world literature, and humanities at Shaw University.*

Oystering

KATHERINE PATERSON

In her novel Jacob Have I Loved, *Katherine Paterson tells the story of Louise Bradshaw, a feisty tomboy growing up on Maryland's Eastern Shore who is filled with envy over the favoritism shown to her twin sister, Caroline. In this excerpt, Louise quits school to start harvesting oysters with her father. The sooks she mentions are female hard crabs; the Jimmies are males.*

It was the last week in November when the first northwest blow of winter sent the egg-laden sooks rushing toward Virginia and the Jimmies deep under the Chesapeake mud. My father took a few days off to shoot duck, and then put the culling board back on the *Portia Sue* and headed out for oysters. One week in school that fall had been enough for me and one week alone on the oyster beds was enough for him. We hardly discussed it. I just got up at two Monday morning, dressed as warmly as I could with a change of clothes in a gunnysack. We ate breakfast together, my mother serving us. No one said anything about my not being a man—maybe they'd forgotten.

I suppose if I were to try to stick a pin through that most elusive spot "the happiest days of my life," that strange winter on the *Portia Sue* with my father would have to be indicated. I was not happy in any way that would make sense to most people, but I was, for the first time in my life, deeply content with what life was giving me. Part of it was the discoveries—who would have believed that my father sang while tonging? My quiet, unassuming father, whose voice could hardly be heard in church, stood there in his oilskins, his rubber-gloved hands on his tongs, and sang to the oysters. It was a wonderful sound, deep and pure. He knew the Methodist hymnbook by heart. "The crabs now, they don't crave music, but oysters," he explained shyly, "there's nothing they favor more than a purty tune." And he would serenade the oysters of Chesapeake Bay with the hymns the brothers Wesley had written to bring sinners to repentance and praise. Part of my deep contentment was due, I'm sure, to being with my father, but part, too, was that I was no longer fighting. My sister was gone, my grandmother a fleeting Sunday apparition, and God, if not dead, far removed from my concern.

It was work that did this for me. I had never had work before that sucked from me every breath, every thought, every trace of energy.

"I wish," said my father one night as we were eating our meager supper in the cabin, "I wish you could do a little studying of a night. You know, keep up your schooling."

We both glanced automatically at the kerosene lamp, which was more smell than light. "I'd be too tired," I said.

"I reckon."

It had been one of our longer conversations. Yet once again I was a member of a good team. We were averaging ten bushels of oysters a day. If it kept up, we'd have a record year. We did not compare ourselves to the skipjacks, the large sailboats with five or six crew members, that raked dredges across the bottom to harvest a heavy load of muck and trash and bottom spat along with oysters each time the mechanical winch cranked up a dredge. We tongers stood perched on the washboards of our tiny boats, and, just as our fathers and grandfathers had before us, used our fir wood tongs, three or four times taller than our own bodies, to reach down gently to the oyster bed, feel the bottom until we came to a patch of market-sized oysters, and then closing the rakes over the catch, bringing it up to the culling board. Of course, we could not help but bring up some spat, as every oyster clings to its bed until the culling hammer forces a separation, but compared to the dredge, we left the precious bottom virtually undisturbed to provide a bed for the oysters that would be harvested by our children's children.

At first, I was only a culler, but if we found a rich bed, I'd tong as well, and then when the culling board was loaded, I'd bring in my last tong full hand over hand, dump it on the board, and cull until I'd caught up with my father.

Oysters are not the mysterious creatures that blue crabs are. You can learn about them more quickly. In a few hours, I could measure a three-inch shell with my eyes. Below three inches they have to go back. A live oyster, a good one, when it hits the culling board has a tightly closed shell. You throw away the open ones. They're dead already. I was a good oyster in those days. Not even the presence at Christmastime of a radiant, grown-up Caroline could get under my shell.

The water began to freeze in late February. I could see my culling like a trail behind us on the quickly forming ice patches. "Them slabs will grow together blessed quick," my father said. And without further discussion, he turned the boat. We stopped only long enough to sell our scanty harvest to a buy boat along the way and then headed straight for Rass. The temperature was dropping fast. By morning we were frozen in tight.

There followed two weeks of impossible weather. My father made no attempt to take the *Portia Sue* out. The first day or so I was content simply to sleep away some of the accumulated exhaustion of the winter. But the day soon came when my mother, handing me a ten o'clock cup of coffee, was suggesting mildly that I might want to take in a few days of school since the bad weather was likely to hold out for some time.

Katherine Paterson *is the award-winning author of many books, including* Jacob Have I Loved, Bridge to Terabithia, *and* Lyddie.

Freeze

Nancy J. Priff

From the failing light and falling mercury,
from his back's cold kinks and the sharp chill in his nose,
the man can tell a freeze is due.
He feels the frigid air settle on long rows of orange trees,
like the late-night hush that falls over hospital beds,
and knows a killing frost is here.

The Weather Service warning came late. Yet he thinks
he should have known, like a mother knows
her toddler has fallen a block away.
He calls on family and friends to protect the fragile fruit.
Under a chilblain moon, they fill and light the age-worn
smudge pots in the shadowy grove.

The man hauls an oil stove to his land's lowest point,
where the cold air sinks, where there's not much hope,
where he fears he is too late.
He plucks a small one, bound for an icy shroud. Cradling it,
he recalls how tiny bud begat fragrant flower and fruit. Shaking
his head, he sighs, "Too young."

A smoky-topaz haze smothers the fields, veiling the
work lights' glare, turning it golden and ghostly. Old men

hold vigil near a radio.
Younger ones wander rows of trees, checking pots,
looking for damage, their predawn mutterings
muffled by the smudgy blanket.

Waiting for a crack in the night's frozen surface,
the man clings to his hope of holding off the cold
till sunrise warms the earth.
He offers a silent prayer for his crop's survival,
lest his family and fields fall victim to the freeze—
like so much tender fruit.

Nancy J. Priff *received a 2003 fellowship from the Pennsylvania Council on the Arts. She has written and edited more than seventy-five videos and dozens of books and supplementary materials on health-care topics. Her poems and short stories have been published in several anthologies. She lives in Ambler, Pennsylvania, with her husband, John Hubbard.*

Legacy

JUNE OWENS

Buried in the ground beneath our feet are remnants of the past—old bones, building foundations, arrowheads, and even prehistoric fossils. As June Owens describes in this essay, fossil hunting can yield great rewards, including revelations about the world that existed millions of years before our own.

On Friday there had been one of those late-winter northeasterly squalls that pound the coastal waterways and river shores of Virginia. With it came the kind of blustery, hard-pelting rain that not only drives a chill into human bones, but chisels away at the soil of the James River cliffs at Claremont and drags it grain by grain into the river's endless flow. Fossil hunting for marine specimens would be at its best, we knew. We would go to Claremont and see what the elements had deposited along the river's edge.

It was still dark when we got up—husband, Harrison, our twelve-year-old son, Patrick, and I. First light was still awhile off. Outside there were no motors. No voices. My breath rose on the stiff air like small ghosts while my eyes adjusted to our unlit suburban surrounds. Saturday, though cold, was starting out splendidly; the ground mists that explore the spaces between the trees—as if looking for something—were already beginning to disperse. We breakfasted well but quickly, munching the last of our toast on the way out to the car. Anxious to get started, we flung knapsacks, light tools, rations for the road, the dogs, and ourselves into our overworked, bright red station wagon. We were on our way to one of our favorite field trip destinations.

An easy day-trip, the drive was less than fifty miles from home. Most of our route ran southeasterly on 10, through Hopewell, then past Burrowsville, with a somewhat sharp northeasterly turn at Cabin Point, beyond Sunken Meadows, and on to Claremont. In those 1960s days, Claremont was no more than a village, lying—usually sun-soaked and breezy in summer, shrouded and full of water echoes in winter—on the western side of the James. In winter there were few visitors, so we could find plenty of working space and little competition from others for what the green clay and limestone cliffs might have given up. What has become of Claremont since, I do not know. I prefer to remember it as it was then, as all good places should be remembered.

The best way to stay warm in cold air is to keep in motion. Young people are better at that than adults, so Patrick padded, zigzagging, ahead. Motion is also important to shoreside fossil hunting. Eyes sweeping the hard-packed sand before us, rucksacks swinging, we waltzed gingerly down the beach. We did not want to damage a valuable find or kick sand over what might be a rare paleontological piece. We kept at a steady advance toward the water. The morning light seemed to have waited for us, for just as we reached that line where earth and water meet, the sun burst forth. The morning was resplendent!

"We should find turritellas today," Patrick announced, referring to his favorite fossil seashell, a beautifully spiral-shaped and sharply pointed gastropod.

"And lots of ecphoras, I hope," Harrison replied. Harrison was especially fond of these golden tan, elegantly ringed prehistoric mollusks.

"I'd settle for a really nice inner ear," I added.

"You already *have* a really nice inner ear," Harrison joked, knowing full well I meant a fossil whale's earbone.

We foraged until almost noon, when the wind picked up. Taking shelter behind the large trunk of a driftwood tree, we rested, sipping scalding tea from thermoses. Patrick had disappeared around a far bend in the shoreline, past a tangle of waterlogged trees that had been ripped up by previous storms from their precarious moorings in the oozing clay overhang. At length, we saw him re-emerge, scrambling back through the mesh of limbs and branches. His legs pumped and his arms waved. But the wind hauled his voice away from us, and we could not hear. I focused instead on Patrick's face. It glowed with excitement. Finally within earshot, his words rang out. He reached us, breathless and red-cheeked, rubbing his cupped hands up and down the front of his windbreaker.

"Hold out your hands and close your eyes. I'll give you something to make you wise," Patrick enjoined, beside himself with animation.

I felt Harrison's hands slip under my upturned ones. When we opened our eyes and saw what our son had brought, our emotions went from disbelief to exhilaration. It was a huge, shining tooth of the Cenozoic giant white shark, *Procarcharodon megalodon!* And it was in perfect condition! The three of us, accompanied by two perplexed but prancing dogs, danced in a circle of happiness.

A mystical bridge had risen to span the space between a boy and the ancient past. Relic from a forty- to fifty-foot long, now extinct shark, the five-inch fossil tooth represented the entire Cenozoic Era. Seventy million years of earth history! At some point within that vast corridor of time, the shark had died. It lay on the bottom of a shallow sea. During the passage of countless centuries, its body disappeared. Neither time nor geologic upheavals, however, could destroy the enormous creature's teeth. One of them had become lodged, pressed between layers of sedimentary soil. Periodic rains over long stretches of years ultimately loosened it from its soft matrix, washing it down to the river's shore.

Afterward, Patrick would cross over the bridge between present and past many times, finding many fine proofs of prehistory. A year later, he would discover a complete cephalopod in Pennsylvania shale. Two years after that he would unearth, in those same Claremont embankments, the fossil remains of a Miocene paddle-swimming marine animal. He would go on field trips with us in numerous states, learn to respect and be considerate of the natural world. But the validation of his curiosity, the freeing of his imagination, came with finding that single, splendid shark tooth. Nothing I know of ever surpassed Patrick's state of utter joy on that morning when he was twelve. The bridge was up. The past had become his legacy, an enduring part of his future.

Born in New York City and raised in Pennsylvania, **June Owens** *now resides in central Florida. Her poems, book reviews, and nonfiction have appeared in many journals and anthologies, including* Atlanta Review, Snowy Egret, *and* Poems of Exotic Places: An Anthology. *She is an ardent earth-lover and environmentalist.*

Digging for Clams

ANINA ROBB

Knee-deep in bay mud
my brother and I dug
and dug the morning
into the day, dug
the sea bottom up
until our hands
were smiling with clams.

Anina Robb *is a writer and teacher living in the Shenandoah Valley of Virginia with her husband, Rob, and their son, Lucas Benjamin. Her poems have been published in a number of different journals. Most recently, her essay "One Step at a Time" was published in a collection by Heinemann, and in August 2002 her poems appeared in* Red River Review *and* Rivendell.

Excerpt from *Mary*

MARY E. MEBANE

*Born in 1933, Mary E. Mebane spent her childhood in rural Durham
County, North Carolina. Her community was a poor one, but, as she describes in this excerpt from her autobiography, berry-picking day was in-
evitably a time of riches.*

It was Friday. Mama didn't have to work tomorrow, and it was
berry-picking time. Berry-picking was a ritual, a part of the
rhythm of summer life. I went to bed, excited.

Mama liked to leave early in the morning, before the sun
got too hot. When I woke up, I reached under the bed and got
my shoes. I hadn't worn them since school let out. They were
my everyday high-tops. My black patent-leather shoes were reserved for Sunday.

Mama put out pots and pans to pick in. She herself used a
water bucket, just like the one that hung in the well. Your sta-
tus in the group was determined by the size of the container
you had. Jesse went sometimes, and he got to carry a water
bucket, too. He was a big boy. I got an aluminum pan. Ruf
Junior got an even smaller one.

I had a glass of cold buttermilk for breakfast, wiped my
mouth with the back of my hand, and ran, for I was afraid that
they might leave without me. All of us went to the road and

joined the other people who were coming down the road on their way to the berry patch, too. We were going Through-the-Woods; that's where the best berries were. I joined the other children in kicking up clouds of dust. Some of them were barefooted, and the wet dew and dust made interesting patterns on their brown feet and legs. But I felt safe because if I stepped on a snake he couldn't bite me through my high-tops.

Mama had on a great straw sundown, and she wore an old dress and her old shoes. She carried a hoe—for snakes. Berry-picking was serious business. She traded a few words with the other women who were going. They carried thick short branches to beat back the bushes and to hit snakes with.

I laughed and ran and kicked up dust with the other children until we got to the path that led through the woods. Then I went streaking ahead through the early-morning dew that glistened on my legs and soaked the tail of my dress. My legs already had two of the biggest dew sores in the crowd, and numerous smaller ones—and I was pleased. (Dew sores were tiny scratches or insect bites that were aggravated if early-morning dew got into them. The dew would keep any sore fresh and could make a new one out of the tiniest scratch.) I knew that when I went back to school I could sit on the rocks at recess and exhibit my sores along with the best of them. Some children had sores so large and so deep that they looked ulcerated. Other children would examine them with awe, and a favored few got to pull off the scabs while everybody crowded around, looking at the red edges and yellow pus inside. Mine never got that big, but I would make up for size with quantity.

It was dark among the trees, different from the road, where the air seemed to shimmer with heat and the houses looked still. I liked to look straight up at the tall pines and wish that I could get up there, to the very top, and sit swaying as the wind blew. But then I tripped on a rock and went sprawling in the grass, got up with dew on my chest, and ran to the next stopping spot.

We didn't know whose berries they were; nobody had heard about the idea of private property. Besides, the berries grew wild—free for everybody. Berry bushes had dark-green vines with whitish flowers and sharp thorns all the way down. If you carefully started picking the ones nearest you, then mashed that plant down with your feet and stood on it so that it couldn't fly back up and scratch you, you could pick the blackberries on the plant a little deeper inside the patch. Soon you would have a little private space all your own. You had to be careful to push the bushes back on the sides, too, or they would fly up and scratch. The grown people picked up high and the children picked down low.

"There's a good patch here," someone shouted.

"Where?" those who didn't have such a promising patch said. Either the berries were still red, which meant that they weren't ripe, or someone had picked the bushes pretty clean the day before.

"Over here," the helpful one announced, and soon the crowd had shifted to another spot. The berries were long and cylindrical; and the blacker they were, the sweeter they were. Some that had started drying up were almost as sweet as candy. We children ate them on the spot, putting purple-stained fingers into our mouths, creating purple-stained tongues, while the grown people wiped sweat and dodged bumblebees.

Sometimes moments passed when there was no sound. That meant everybody had a "good" spot and was concentrating on filling a container. The grown people's containers didn't make a noise, for they quickly covered the bottom. The children plunked each individual berry into their pans, and each berry would go *plunk, plunk, plunk*. Sometimes the noise never stopped, for before the berries covered the bottom, they would have eaten the contents and would have to start over again, only to finish the day with the bottom of the container showing through the fruit.

"Yon he go!" someone yelled.

"Where? Where?" everybody shouted. They didn't need to ask what. It was a snake. The grown people reached for their sticks. Mama reached for the hoe. And the scared snake slithered away just as fast as he could. The excitement died down and berry-picking resumed.

I picked and ate and picked and ate, but I was a little unhappy; I wanted to fill my pot up to the top, yet I wanted to eat like the other children. But I wanted a full pot so that Mama would praise me. The other children didn't seem to care whether they filled their pots, and their mothers didn't care, either, except to say now and then, "Get out of my way, child, before I step on you."

When the sun got hot and all the grown people were wet with sweat, their dresses clinging to their arms and little rivers of sweat running down their necks, they murmured among themselves and we left the berry patch. Most of the children had pan showing through the berries; mine was three layers deep in berries, but my tongue was stained a deep purple.

"Get the jars," Mama said when we got home.

Ruf Junior and I went to the smokehouse to get last year's jars. They were sticky with the residue from the canning last year. Mama never washed them before putting them away.

Other women did, but she didn't. I never have been able to figure out why; perhaps it never occurred to her.

We came out, carrying half-gallon Mason jars with heavy gray lids on them. The lids had glass inside. If the glass wasn't cracked, we would use the lid again. If it was cracked we would throw that top away, for it would cause the food to spoil.

Mama was already down in the yard, lighting a fire around the washpot. We drew buckets of water from the well and poured it into the washpot. Then we got the washtubs and filled them half full of water. When the water in the washpot boiled, Mama poured hot water into the half-filled tubs and put a hunk of lye soap in. I liked to stir it around and around until the water got cloudy and started to suds up.

I washed jar after jar, putting my hands down in the water to the elbow and scrubbing at the ridges on top where last year's berry stains remained. Ruf Junior washed the tops. Then we rinsed them in a smaller tub and set them up to dry. They were ready to be filled with the berries that we had picked.

In the kitchen Mama washed the berries through bucket after bucket of water and picked them. Then there was a small mountain of sugar that she poured in on top of them. I watched while the small mountain slowly dissolved and made the berries on top turn crusty white.

Before the berries cooked, I started to itch. "Chiggers," Mama said. I knew to get the kerosene. A chigger was hiding down under my skin, and he had raised bumps all over me. I tried to scratch him, but my skin got between me and him. But he didn't like kerosene and that would stop him.

It did for a while. But then he started itching again and I had to put more kerosene on him. He wasn't in my navel. If he got down in your navel he had won, for you couldn't reach him, and he stayed there and itched so bad that you couldn't sleep that night.

I rubbed all over in kerosene, and by the time Mama had started to pour the heavy blackberry liquid into the half-gallon jars, I had gone to bed.

～

Mary E. Mebane *attended college and graduate school in North Carolina, earning her Ph.D. in English from the University of North Carolina. She taught at the University of South Carolina and the University of Wisconsin—Milwaukee. Her two autobiographies are* Mary *and* Mary, Wayfarer.

Seven Haiku

Lenard D. Moore

a crow lands
on the cell phone tower
evening heat

a shirtless man
fishing in the rip tide—
the smell of salt

family night
the referee's shadow
walks toward midfield

starry night
only one pine lit
by the billboard

breezy night
a small praying mantis
on the side mirror

new year's night
my wife leaves
to pick up her mother

a childhood song
along the rural road—
falling star

Lenard D. Moore *was born in Jacksonville, North Carolina. He is the author of* Desert Storm: A Brief History *and* Forever Home. *Twice nominated for the Pushcart Prize, he has written poems, essays, and reviews for more than 350 publications. He teaches English, world literature, and humanities at Shaw University.*

The Eco-Canoeist

SY MONTGOMERY

Many people devote considerable time to caring for the natural world. They plant trees, rescue injured animals, create parks, and clean up beaches. Who are these people with such a strong commitment to stewardship? Sometimes they're not at all who you'd expect.

In the thirteen years Dale Hatch has worked as a ranger at Jay Blanchard Park in Orlando, he's seen some wonderful and strange things. It's a gem of an urban park, where among the cypress, afternoon calls of barred owls nearly drown out the highway noise. The tea-colored Little Econlohatchee River flows through the park's 412 acres, and brings with it herons, wood ducks, otters, egrets, ibis, sandhill cranes, and stinkpot and painted turtles, as well as 484,000 human visitors. You can catch a thirteen-pound largemouth bass here—but the health department warns you to eat fish from the Little Econ only once a week. There's mercury in the river, though no one is sure where it comes from.

You can find some weird stuff in the river, Hatch says: everything from trousers to toilets. The Little Econ drains dozens of housing developments, he says, and after a flood, you can find trash four and five feet up in the trees. But about a decade ago, Hatch and the other rangers noticed something

really strange. The trash started disappearing from the water. They would find muddy garbage piling up inside park trash cans. "We couldn't figure out where in the world it was coming from," Hatch says in his Florida drawl. "Somebody was pulling this stuff up out of the river. We didn't know how, but we were sure glad whoever it was was doing it."

For months, as the rangers emptied the trash cans, they wondered who would do such a thing. Then one day, paddling in a canoe piled high with wet garbage was a person Hatch recognized. They'd first met on the park's soccer field some months before. Six feet tall and muscled, the stranger was dressed in fatigues, working out beside a maroon van plastered with Marines bumper stickers, practicing martial arts moves with a weapon that looked like nunchakus. At the time, Hatch remembers, he thought, "Uh-oh."

Hatch never suspected that, like Clark Kent, this thirty-four-year-old ex-Marine had an alter ego: the Eco-Canoeist. For more than a decade, few others suspected it either. Unrecognized, unfunded, and usually alone, Steve Nordlinger takes every spare moment, loads his canoe into his van, puts in at waterways around the state, and pursues a goal most people would consider too huge to even try: to clean up, by hand, hundreds of thousands of miles of Florida's rivers, lakes, swamps, canals, and ocean.

It's not just a dirty job, but a dangerous one. Sodden river garbage is unwieldy—a truck tire can weigh well over a hundred pounds when it's filled with mud and water, and somehow you have to lift it into your canoe without capsizing. He's hoisted out refrigerators, car parts, boat wreckage, picnic tables, dog houses, sofas. But it's the little stuff—the stuff anyone can lift—that arguably does the most harm. Birds choke on fishing line. Turtles die eating Styrofoam. Ordinary rope strangles manatees. Removing brittle, rusty cans and the barbs of discarded fishing gear, Steve's cut his own flesh open again and again. But he keeps at it. By his own conservative estimate, he has single-handedly removed 240 tons of trash and fishing line from the state's waterways.

Hatch recalls his astonishment at the feat. "I could not believe that one person would go out on his own and do something like that—nobody asked him, nobody's paying him, he wasn't even telling us about it so we could praise him," said the ranger. "So we had to catch him accidentally—catch him cleanin' up our river!"

Steve seems like a superhero straight out of a comic book. In fact, his exploits have now been recorded in a comic book format: five volumes of *The Eco-Canoeist's Journal*—hand-drawn, hand-lettered, hand-xeroxed, and hand-delivered to bookstores around the state—detail his trash collecting adventures and methods. His work has attracted the attention of local press and national radio, the praise of county commissioners, and the dedication of so large a group of volunteers that there aren't enough canoes to hold them all—not even with the three new ones that now bring Steve's fleet of canoes to ten, thanks to a small grant recently garnered from Disney.

The Eco-Canoeist is a strange kind of superhero. He's a lethally potent fighter, yet so gentle he scrapes loose and releases the snails anchored inside the tin cans he picks up out of rivers. He's a Mother Teresa of Florida wildlife, dressed in Marines fatigues. He is part Don Quixote and part Superman. But he is also, in important ways, an ordinary person—with an extraordinary will.

Sy Montgomery has been chased by an angry silverback gorilla in Zaire, bitten by a vampire bat in Costa Rica, and hunted by a tiger in India. She's lived these and other adventures while researching her many articles and books, including The Snake Scientist, Encantando: Pink Dolphin of the Amazon, *and* Search for the Golden Moon Bear: Science and Adventure in the Asian Tropics.

Wild Lives

Tiger of the Air

KATHARINE CRAWFORD ROBEY

The Piedmont region of Georgia may not have the wild drama of the mountains or the coast. But in its gently rolling landscape, one can find fields, forests, and even backyards where remarkable wild creatures scratch out their existence.

I climb into the high awkward bed that's mine for two weeks and watch the pine trees sway. My parents, wildlife biologists, are doing fieldwork in the peaks of the north Georgia mountains. My friends are back home on the Savannah coast. I'm stuck in between in Atlanta—no mountains or beach, just rolling, dull hills—and Great Aunt Beulah.

"Good night, Warren." Her voice quavers outside my door. The floorboards shake as she leaves. I press my eyelids shut and picture home. The noisy trip through Atlanta rises up—the huge roaring highway, a ride on the subway, MARTA, floating on a narrow track above tons of traffic, swishing underground through dark, carved stone. My eyes snap open. I get out of bed, go to the small desk below the window, and begin to write:

Friday, February 15, 1991 (Dismal)
Getting off MARTA, concrete and honking cars surrounded me. But in Great Aunt's neighborhood there's nothing but tall

pines and oaks. What did Great Aunt call Atlanta, the city of trees? There are so many that I feel completely closed in. On the coast the sky is everywhere. It's cold here, even in the house. Great Aunt's big on wearing sweaters. She's knitting one now. I can hear her needles click. But another sound comes suddenly to me from outside, a low moan. Now a higher, more anxious call. What wild sounding thing could possibly live in a big city?

Monday, three days later (Stormy)

It's been raining ever since I got here. Last night there was a huge storm. The pines tossed and the rubbery magnolia shook. The only other sound besides the rain is the constant tap of Great Aunt's knitting needles. The phone never even rings. Great Aunt doesn't use it so no one calls her back. I'm at the desk in my room doing homework. (Was that a streak of brown flying across the yard just now? Maybe not.) I've figured out that Great Aunt is eight times my own age. There's nothing to say to her. I can't wait to go home.

Later on Monday (Something finally happens)

This afternoon I found an amazing creature under the tallest pine in the yard. It's a huge baby bird, downy white with piercing yellow eyes with huge black pupils, small wings, and big black feet. The black skin around his eyes gives him the look of a monkey or maybe a baboon. Great Aunt actually stopped knitting when she saw him and threw up her hands. We put the oversized chick on a towel in a box by the oven to get warm and dry—and fed him the leftover liver from last night. (I'm glad he likes it. I certainly didn't.) He's totally unafraid of us.

At dinner Great Aunt broke the silence. "With his curved-down beak and big eyes he must be an owlet, the baby of a very large owl." A large owl, in the middle of the city? Whatever he is, he's the oddest cute-looking bird I've ever seen.

Tuesday (Bitter cold but dry)

A big day. This morning in the tallest pine tree I saw what must be the owlet's parent! I got Great Aunt's binoculars and zoomed in on him—or her. It's a very large brownish gray bird, maybe two feet tall. It has very long ear tufts that stick straight up. The bird swiveled its head almost completely around and blinked down at me with huge amber eyes. And below it I saw a large scramble of twigs and dry leaves—the nest.

"I don't want to put you back, baby owl," I said to the owlet in the kitchen. "But you're wild and need to go home."

Halfway up the ladder to the owl's nest I lost my nerve. I had the owlet inside my jacket. He was calm and safe. But what if I fell? What if his parents came and dive-bombed me with their claws? My legs started to tremble. The whole ladder shook. Suddenly Great Aunt appeared below and steadied it. With each step I took she told me, "No owls in sight." The owlet nestled against me warmly. I finally reached the large nest. What a surprise—two more owlets are inside it! I placed mine carefully between them, and gave his soft head one last pat. He gurgled at me. When I got down I looked up and saw all three owlets bob up above the rim of the nest. Mine's the biggest.

Tonight at dinner I broke the silence. "They're great horned owls," I said. "I looked it up. They eat mice, rats, and chipmunks, and nest in winter. I think I heard them call the first night I came. They hoot."

"Ah," Great Aunt said. "The hoot owl. Also called the tiger of the air."

"I carried a tiger back to his nest!" I said.

The phone rang then and we both jumped. It was my parents.

Thursday (Still bitter)

I hurried out to the owl nest but no owl was sitting on it, no owls anywhere. I clucked to the owlets, but they didn't bob up or gurgle back. How long can they last without the warmth and food of their parents?

Evening came. More cold rain. How could any owlet survive this? I borrowed my great aunt's raincoat and went out. By the streetlight I could see through the haze. Two ear tufts stuck out of the nest and a long body—the mother owl has returned! She's keeping the owlets dry. With her tufts and soft looking body she reminds me of a large Persian cat. I saw the father, too. He's keeping watch on a branch above the nest. He hooted and his broad tail moved up and down.

Saturday (Finally sunny)

A week left. This afternoon Great Aunt drove us down Piedmont Road to get something for dinner. Traffic was noisy. The sun glinted off the hoods of the cars.

"Would you like more liver?" she said, squinting in the slanting light.

I had an answer ready. "How about spaghetti?" I blurted out. "I'll help you make it!" At dinner Great Aunt said our spaghetti was the best she'd ever tasted. Now all we need to know is whether the owlet is getting enough to eat. The

mother owl is staying on the nest all the time, the father keeps watch above. They never seem to feed their babies.

P.S. When I brought the spaghetti to the table, there on my chair was the sweater Great Aunt's been working on so hard. It's cream and brown with a streak of blue. I'm wearing it over my pajamas right now and I'm finally warm all the way through.

Sunday night (Bright moonlight)

As I was lying in bed I heard hooting. I got up and opened my window part way to hear better. I saw a shadowy owl fly silently across the yard. He had something in his talons! When the owl reached the nest the owlets squawked. Then more hooting and loud squawking. I stood listening to the happy racket.

"Good night, Warren," Great Aunt whispered through the door.

"The tigers of the air are hunting," I said. "Come in and hear them." She entered my room for the first time since I've been here. We let the owls do the talking. Finally she said, "They sound like a real family." She's right. When Mom and Dad and I have dinner together, it's noisy like that. Dinners with Great Aunt aren't noisy. But now we have the owls to talk about.

Wednesday (Cloudy but warmer)

Great Aunt and I haven't seen the owlets bob up under their mother for three days. Often she leaves the nest for long stretches of time. We've both been worried. Were the owlets sick? We got out the ladder again. I made it up and was about to peek into the nest when Great Aunt cried, "Watch out!"

I froze against the tree. Out of the corner of my eye I saw two huge owls appear. They rattled their beaks against the tree trunk and swooped close to me. They hooted soft and low and barked, almost exactly like dogs. But they didn't attack. Maybe they know I'm a friend.

I took a quick peek into the nest. The owlets are fine! They're growing, especially mine. He's turned from white to brown and white, and his wings are long. But he still has a quizzical expression in his eyes, as if he's asking me a question. Suddenly I want to stay in Atlanta and watch the owlet grow up. My parents, though, come in just three days.

Thursday (Partly cloudy)

This morning as every morning I checked on the owlet—but today I asked Great Aunt to come along. The mother was off the nest, on an upper branch. When I clucked, the owlet peered down at me and loudly cried, *Mee-eeep! Mee-eeep!* He doesn't gurgle like a baby anymore. How I'll miss him!

Friday (Sunny and warm)

I see now that although the trees block much of the sky, it's because of them that the owlet is here, and his parents. Tigers of the air need lots of trees to live in. Now instead of making me feel closed in, they make me feel cozy and protected like the sweater Great Aunt knit me.

Great Aunt and I checked on the owlet one last time together. He was standing on the rim of the nest, flapping his awesome wings. Using his claws and beak like a parrot, he clambered out and up to a branch.

"Fly, tiger of the air!" I called.

The owlet lifted his wings, stared down, folded his wings in again, and climbed back inside the nest. He peered at me in a questioning way.

"He doesn't trust his wings," I said to my great aunt. "I leave tomorrow. I won't get to see the owlet fly. What if he never does?"

"When you were a baby I saw you crawl," she said. "But I missed the moment when you walked." She put her heavy arm around me.

"Then how did you know that I did it?" I asked.

"Ah," she said. "The telephone."

Saturday (Changeable weather)

Cool air from the mountains sweeps across Great Aunt's yard, making amazing cloud shadows. By the time the air reaches the coast it will be soft and warm. My parents just came. I must pack my pen.

As I walk Mom and Dad over to the owl tree, I talk of Atlanta and liver and trees and owls and my great Great Aunt. We're leaving the hills that aren't dull after all and going home. But on the day the owlet flies Great Aunt's promised me that she'll pick up the telephone and tell me all about it. I can't wait.

Katharine Crawford Robey *lives in Atlanta, Georgia, where she writes stories and novels for young people.*

Swifts at Evening

JEFFREY HARRISON

The whoosh of rush hour traffic washes through my head
as I cross the bridge through the treetops into my neighborhood
and what's left of my thoughts is sucked up suddenly
by a huge whirlwind of birds, thousands of chimney swifts
wheeling crazily overhead against a sky just beginning
to deepen into evening—turning round and round
in their erratic spiral ragged at the edges
where more chittering birds join in the circling
flock from every direction, having spent all
day on the wing scattered for miles across
September skies and now pulled into the
great vortex that funnels into the air-
shaft of the library, the whole day
going like water down a drain with
the sucking sound of traffic and
the birds swirling like specks
of living sediment drawn from
the world into the whirlpool
into the word-pool flapping
like bats at the last
moment diving and
turning into
words.

Jeffrey Harrison *is the author of three collections of poetry,* The
Singing Underneath, Signs of Arrival, *and* Feeding the Fire. *He
lives in Massachusetts with his wife, son, and daughter.*

Alligators

WILLIAM BARTRAM

*In the latter decades of the 1700s, naturalist William Bartram jour-
neyed through the Southeast, recording the plants, animals, and places
he encountered. One evening he set up camp beside a river that, he soon
discovered, was brimming over with alligators. Bartram nonetheless
rowed into the river to catch a fish for dinner. Then, after returning to his
campsite, he witnessed this remarkable scene.*

It was by this time dusk, and the alligators had nearly ceased
their roar, when I was again alarmed by a tumultuous noise
that seemed to be in my harbour, and therefore engaged my
immediate attention. Returning to my camp, I found it undisturbed, and then continued on to the extreme point of the
promontory, where I saw a scene, new and surprising, which at
first threw my senses into such a tumult, that it was some time
before I could comprehend what was the matter; however, I
soon accounted for the prodigious assemblage of crocodiles at
this place, which exceeded every thing of the kind I had ever
heard.

How shall I express myself so as to convey an adequate idea
of it to the reader, and at the same time avoid raising suspi-
cions of my veracity. Should I say that the river (in this place)
from shore to shore, and perhaps near half a mile above and

below me, appeared to be one solid bank of fish, of various kinds, pushing through this narrow pass of St. Juan's into the little lake, on their return down the river, and that the alligators were in such incredible numbers, and so close together from shore to shore, that it would have been easy to have walked across on their heads, had the animals been harmless? What expressions can sufficiently declare the shocking scene that for some minutes continued, whilst this mighty army of fish were forcing the pass? During this attempt, thousands, I may say hundreds of thousands, of them were caught and swallowed by the devouring alligators. I have seen an alligator take up out of the water several great fish at a time, and just squeeze them betwixt his jaws, while the tails of the great trout flapped about his eyes and lips, ere he had swallowed them. The horrid noise of their closing jaws, their plunging amidst the broken banks of fish, and rising with their prey some feet upright above the water, the floods of water and blood rushing out of their mouths, and the clouds of vapour issuing from their wide nostrils were truly frightful. This scene continued at intervals during the night, as the fish came to the pass. After this sight, shocking and tremendous as it was, I found myself somewhat easier and more reconciled to my situation; being convinced that their extraordinary assemblage here was owing to this annual feast of fish; and that they were so well employed in their own element, that I had little occasion to fear their paying me a visit.

William Bartram *was born in Philadelphia in 1739. Devoted to the study of natural history, he made a journey of thousands of miles around the American Southeast to document the region's animal and botanical resources. The resulting book,* Travels, *heightened European interest in the American wilderness. Bartram was known from then on as a leading authority on plants and birds, and was even asked by Thomas Jefferson to join the Lewis and Clark expedition of the West, an invitation he declined due to health issues. He died in 1823.*

Whooping Cranes

MARJORIE KINNAN RAWLINGS

Marjorie Kinnan Rawlings's novel The Yearling *introduces readers to a boy named Jody who lives in Florida's big scrub country in the 1930s. His is a wild region where deer and bears and panthers still live in relative abundance. In this excerpt, Jody and his father, Penny, are winding up a day of fishing when they witness the dramatic dance of whooping cranes, birds that are today extremely rare.*

Jody put the small fish back reluctantly and watched it swim away. His father was stern about not taking more of anything, fish or game, than could be eaten or kept. Hope of another monster dwindled as the sun finished its spring arc of the daylight sky. He cast leisurely, taking his pleasure in his increasing dexterity of arm and wrist. The moon was now wrong. It was no longer feed-time. The fish were not striking. Suddenly he heard his father whistle like a quail. It was the signal they used together in squirrel hunting. Jody laid down his pole and looked back to make sure he could identify the tuft of grass where he had covered his bass from the rays of the sun. He walked cautiously to where his father beckoned.

Penny whispered, "Foller me. We'll ease up clost as we dare."
He pointed. "The whoopin' cranes is dancin'."
Jody saw the great white birds in the distance. His father's

eye, he thought, was like an eagle's. They crouched on all fours and crept forward slowly. Now and then Penny dropped flat on his stomach and Jody dropped behind him. They reached a clump of high saw-grass and Penny motioned for concealment behind it. The birds were so close that it seemed to Jody he might touch them with his long fishing pole. Penny squatted on his haunches and Jody followed. His eyes were wide. He made a count of the whooping cranes. There were sixteen.

The cranes were dancing a cotillion as surely as it was danced at Volusia. Two stood apart, erect and white, making a strange music that was part cry and part singing. The rhythm was irregular, like the dance. The other birds were in a circle. In the heart of the circle, several moved counter-clock-wise. The musicians made their music. The dancers raised their wings and lifted their feet, first one and then the other. They sunk their heads deep in their snowy breasts, lifted them and sunk again. They moved soundlessly, part awkwardness, part grace. The dance was solemn. Wings fluttered, rising and falling like out-stretched arms. The outer circle shuffled around and around. The group in the center attained a slow frenzy.

Suddenly all motion ceased. Jody thought the dance was over, or that the intruders had been discovered. Then the two musicians joined the circle. Two others took their places. There was a pause. The dance was resumed. The birds were reflected in the clear marsh water. Sixteen white shadows reflected the motions. The evening breeze moved across the saw-grass. It bowed and fluttered. The water rippled. The setting sun lay rosy on the white bodies. Magic birds were dancing in a mystic marsh. The grass swayed with them, and the shallow waters, and the earth fluttered under them. The earth was dancing with the cranes, and the low sun, and the wind and sky.

Jody found his own arms lifting and falling with his breath, as the cranes' wings lifted. The sun was sinking into the saw-grass. The marsh was golden. The whooping cranes were washed with gold. The far hammocks were black. Darkness came to the lily pads, and the water blackened. The cranes were whiter than any clouds, or any white bloom of oleander or of lily. Without warning, they took flight. Whether the hour-long dance was, simply, done, or whether the long nose of an alligator had lifted above the water to alarm them, Jody could not tell, but they were gone. They made a great circle against the sunset, whooping their strange rusty cry that sounded only in their flight. Then they flew in a long line into the west, and vanished.

Penny and Jody straightened and stood up. They were cramped from the long crouching. Dusk lay over the saw-grass, so that the ponds were scarcely visible. The world was shadow, melting into shadow. They turned to the north. Jody found his bass. They cut to the east, to leave the marsh behind them, then north again. The trail was dim in the growing darkness. It joined the scrub road and they turned once more east, continuing now in a certainty, for the dense growth of the scrub bordered the road like walls. The scrub was black and the road was a dark gray strip of carpet, sandy and soundless. Small creatures darted across in front of them and scurried in the bushes. In the distance, a panther screamed. Bull-bats shot low over their heads. They walked in silence.

At the house, bread was baked and waiting, and hot fat was in the iron skillet. Penny lighted a fat-wood torch and went to the lot to do his chores. Jody scaled and dressed the fish at the back stoop, where a ray of light glimmered from the fire on the hearth. Ma Baxter dipped the pieces in meal and fried them crisp and golden. The family ate without speaking.

She said, "What ails you fellers?"

They did not answer. They had no thought for what they ate nor for the woman. They were no more than conscious that she spoke to them. They had seen a thing that was unearthly. They were in a trance from the strong spell of its beauty.

⁓◞⁓

Born in 1896, **Marjorie Kinnan Rawlings** *moved to northern Florida in 1928 to write fiction. Her best known works include* Cross Creek, *a memoir, and* The Yearling, *the Pulitzer Prize-winning novel. Rawlings's home is now a historic state park and is still home to many of Florida's wild species.*

Gopher Tortoise Lament

ANN MORROW

I didn't invite them,
But they came anyway:
Tick and spider;
Cricket and beetle;
Frog and toad.

I didn't encourage them,
But they stayed anyway:
Bird and box turtle;
Mouse and raccoon;
Snake and skunk.

So this is what we all do:

When fire comes
Racing through wiregrass,
Drinking pine pitch and
Spitting flames,
We go down.
Deep, where it feels cool,
Safe.

When frost comes
Riding bitter winds,
Howling and dancing
At the burrow entrance,
We go down.
Deep, where it feels warm,
Safe.

I didn't invite them,
But we live together anyway:
Fur and scale;
Whisker and scute;
Wing and fang.

Note: Giant tick, scarab beetle, Eastern diamondback rattlesnake, and burrowing owl—these are just some of the more than three hundred organisms that find food and shelter within the deep burrows of the gopher tortoise, an unwitting landlord in some of Florida's

upland habitats. We can only speculate on how many of these species may occupy a burrow at any one time or about the predator-prey relationships within the close confines of a burrow. We do know that several of the burrow residents, such as the gopher frog, Eastern indigo snake, Florida pine snake, and Florida mouse, are protected species in Florida, as is, of course, the gopher tortoise.

Ann Morrow *has been writing about Florida's wildlife in magazines, books, and newspapers since 1984. She coauthored, with Susan Cerulean, the* Florida Wildlife Viewing Guide *and* Florida Trails: A Guide to Florida's Natural Habitats. *A biologist by training, she lives with her husband and two children in Tallahassee, Florida.*

Potomac and
the Gray Swan

DAY ALEXANDER

Across the Potomac River from downtown Washington, D.C., lies Theodore Roosevelt Island. Here the river divides in two as it sweeps around the long, forested island and southward to the Chesapeake Bay. In early days, when no white person had yet ventured near this region, the river's banks were home to Indian villages. It is from this ancient time that the following legend comes. Some of the titles it carries in old newspapers include "The Legend of Potomac," "The Gray Swan," and "How the Potomac Was Named." Storyteller Day Alexander calls it "Potomac and the Gray Swan."

~~~

She was named Potomac by her father, because on the morning of her birth, a flock of swans had flown down to the river, landing on the island opposite the village. Potomac meant *swan* in her family's language.

Where no swans had settled before, now there were hundreds. The father took this as a powerful omen, and that is why he named his daughter after the swans. From that time forward, swans flew in from the northland each fall, crying out their cries, swooping down to the forested island.

Each spring when the flowers burst out in the forest, the swans left, one flying behind the other to the northland. So winter followed fall, and summer followed spring. The swans flew away and came back. In those seasons, the girl Potomac grew up from baby to child to girl to young woman.

When the swans dwelt on the island, Potomac walked down to the river's edge to look at them. She stepped over large stones to reach the island. On a flat rock she sat and watched the swans swim and nibble on the marsh grasses.

Amongst the wild swans was one gray swan who was larger than the rest. He was the leader, and when he flew up the others followed. When he cried out, they repeated his cry. When Potomac sat on the rock in the forest, it was this swan who swam near her.

"Does he know that my name is Potomac, too—the same name as his?" she wondered.

One night Potomac had this dream: She dreamed that she was on the island. On the rock lay the gray swan, one of his great wings twisted and broken.

The swan lifted his head and said to Potomac, "Find the red reed that grows in the marshes. Its juice will heal me."

In the dream, Potomac had looked down at herself and saw that she, too, was a swan. She flew over the marsh, searching for the red reed. Finding one and carrying it in her beak, she returned to the rock and let the red juice flow onto the wing. The gray swan's wing healed. Up he flew, circling over the island.

Potomac awoke from her dream. She found herself in her own sleeping place in her father's lodge. But the dream was so strong in her memory that she quietly left the lodge as her family slept, and crept down to the river's edge and crossed over to the island.

In the glow of the moonlight she saw the gray swan lying on the flat rock. His eyes regarded hers for a moment and then closed. Potomac knew what to do. Swiftly she waded into the marsh, pushing reeds aside until she found one of red, glistening like heart's blood.

Potomac broke off the reed and brought it to the gray swan, who was panting short breaths. She carefully laid the reed on the broken wing. The gray swan looked at her. The wing did not heal. Then she remembered that in her dream, she had carried the reed in her beak.

Seizing the reed, Potomac bit off the stems and chewed. With her hands she cupped this juice onto the wing. Before her eyes, the wing healed. The gray swan flexed his wings and flew up from the rock. He circled around her.

Potomac watched him as he flew across the moon.

Each morning thereafter, Potomac found a gray swan feather at the entrance

to her father's lodge. When she had enough, she sewed a dress of swan feathers.

Spring came. The swans flew away to the northland. As the swans followed their ways, so Potomac followed hers. Each day she put on her tunic of swan feathers and stepped over to the island. She sat on the flat rock where the gray swan had lain, remembering her dream, holding it close to her, waiting for him to return.

One fall day when the red and yellow leaves of the trees blew in the wind, the swans returned. Potomac saw them high in the sky, then circling down to the island. The gray swan cried his wild cry as he landed on the water.

On the same day, Potomac's father called her to his side.

"My daughter," her father said, "in the village, the chief's son has expressed his desire to marry you. At the full moon, you and he will wed."

Potomac looked at him in wonderment. "I do not love this young man. Please, Father, allow me to choose my own husband."

Her father shook his head. "He is the chief's son. I cannot deny him."

That night Potomac left her father's lodge. She crept to the river bank and crossed over to the island. On the flat rock she knelt. "Oh, help me, Gray Swan, as once I helped you."

She looked into the forest where the trees whispered together. As she looked, a stranger emerged out of the shadows. He was tall and straight as a forest tree. "Who are you? From where did you come?" she asked.

"I am from the north," he replied.

Potomac loved him from that moment. And the stranger loved her. Each night they met by the flat rock as the moon grew to its fullness. They made their plans to leave the village by the river before Potomac was to marry.

They did not notice that they were followed. The chief's son crept behind trees and watched them. He, too, made a plan.

On the night before the full moon, Potomac gathered her belongings. In her dress of swan feathers, she left her father's lodge and crossed the stepping stones over to the island.

By the flat rock she saw her lover. An arrow pierced his chest, but he was breathing.

"Find the red reed," he whispered.

Potomac, swift as a deer, waded into the marsh, searching for the red reed. At last she found one stalk, red as heart's blood. She chewed on it as she ran back to the rock and pulled out the arrow. Cupping the juice of the reed into her hands, she poured it on the wound. The wound healed.

Potomac looked into the gray eyes of the stranger. So this is who he is, she thought. She smiled at him. Together they leapt from the rock as they became gray swans. Up, up they flew, crying out to the other swans, who followed them into the sky, repeating the cries.

The swans did not return to the island. In hopes that they would, the river was named the Potomac.

When **Day Alexander** *was a school librarian with the D.C. public schools, she collected old legends of the place for storytelling. Her published works include* The Legend of the Treaty Oak, A Forgotten Tale of Washington, D.C., The Gift to the Selkie, *and* Jump, Clap, and Sing: Singing Games of Washington, D.C., Children.

Green Heron

Ann E. Michael

Past the bay's canals we reached inlets
where osprey dive and nest, preen
using wind as a comb.
You looked into the water,
counted jellyfish drifting
like cellophane coins in brine
beneath the canoe: 36, 37, 38—
I sat in the stern, looking over your head,
thinking, soon you will be
tall as a man.
You feathered your paddle along
the surface aglint with ordinary reflections.
It was then I spied the green heron,
all legs and beak.
"Like me," you laughed, as the Chesapeake
deepened itself around us.

Ann E. Michael *lives in eastern Pennsylvania. She is a 1998 recipient of a poetry fellowship from the Pennsylvania Council on the Arts and a contributor of poetry and essays to many literary journals and anthologies.*

Our Lads

JAKE PAGE

Trying to save an orphaned baby bird is a difficult task, and one that far too often ends in defeat. Still, many of us can't help but try, compelled by our parental instincts, or perhaps by the image of some imagined future day when the bird, now strong and hardy, lifts off for its first taste of flight.

This is a story of a crime.

They arrived one July in a disreputable sprawl of skin and bone, clinging to a dark and sooty nest in the fireplace. *Chaetura pelagica,* chimney swifts—common enough arrivals in the affairs of human beings through some inefficiency of their species in fastening nests to the insides of chimneys. Featherless infants squalling for parental care, sounding like locusts. Four of them—one dead and the others more than likely doomed. The odds in life may be six-to-five against, but with orphaned baby birds the odds are infinitely worse.

As usual, Susanne went immediately to the rescue, plunging herself into the unknown exigencies of chimney swift motherhood. The creatures were gathered up, nasty nest and all, and put into a cardboard carton, while I headed for the bookshelf.

Insectivorous birds: Therefore the first step was to puree

beef, add a touch of water and a little milk for calcium and, with an eyedropper, stick the puree into three open beaks. Chimney swifts are among the hardest bird orphans to feed because of their infernal head waggling. A miss here, a successful squirt there, and in a few minutes the screeching subsided. A chancy beginning.

Every hour they squalled and the puree was applied. Swifts fledge in thirty days. When did they hatch? Since they were featherless on arrival, we assume less than a week ago. Three weeks of dawn-to-dusk hourly feeding?

A few days passed and the birds began to show signs of feathers—follicles and fluff. The feathers came and the birds gained in size. I read up on the swifts. They are, like everything under the sun, wonderful beings, however little we know of their lives. Assuming for the moment that the babies survived, they would be capable of flight clocked at up to thirty-five miles per hour. They would spend virtually all day in flight, soaring and swooping, batlike, after insects such as beetles and flying ants and airborne spiders. In the best of circumstances, these ragamuffin infants could live for fourteen years, during which time they could fly as many as a million and a half miles.

After a week, the babies' eyes opened and they stared at their mother with a total lack of expression, yelling for food. Imagine finding that your mother is about a thousand times bigger than you. An impossible standard.

Swifts are gregarious, roosting in groups of up to ten thousand, descending an hour after sunset into huge industrial chimneys like clouds of smoke in reverse action. They inhabit much of eastern North America in spring and summer, and winter in the upper Amazon basin in Brazil and Peru. Brazil? Peru?

This feeding is hopeless, we think. One gets its bill stuck shut, being sloppy with the puree. *Sturm und Drang* as warm water is applied. Another small crisis resolved. They continued to grow, turning sooty dark; short, stubby bills frowned at us, gibbety-gibbety, demanding. They traveled with us in the car as much as a hundred miles without protest.

When it was time for them to fledge, we learned, they would be able to fly across the room. We should then put them, the experts said, on a telephone pole. They'd climb to the top and take off. But where would they go at night? By even contemplating such questions, we realized we had reached the point where maybe the odds were only six-to-five against.

After about two more days, the swifts took to popping out of the wicker basket that early on had replaced their altogether disreputable hovel of a nest. They would hop onto Susanne's shirt, glaring like three upside-down bats, then climb upward into her blonde hair. Sharp, spiny tail feather tips stuck out like a comb, the swift's equivalent of a mountaineer's crampons. Little needles that could make you wince, but just the thing for clinging to the side of a chimney or to a surrogate mother.

Would they know about catching insects? Susanne swatted flies and occasionally substituted them, or mealworms, for the beef. They liked the beef better.

On the seventeenth day, Susanne bore them outdoors clinging to her shirt. It was a windy day, with the sun peering out between mountainous clouds. The birds climbed onto her head. They looked expressionlessly at the world. Overhead chimney swifts soared and swooped, along with barn swallows and purple martins. We thought it might do these preschoolers some good to have a glimpse of their ultimate role, but seeing the athletic grace going on overhead, we believed that there was no way our orphans would be equal to it.

At which point, one of the swifts, the one that had a suggestion of eagle in its countenance (or so we thought) and that had refused a morning meal that day, took off from Susanne's head. It flew low over our yard and the next, headed for a large tree, swerved, and sailed up into the clouded sky. The wild swifts gathered around, flying with it, soaring on scimitar wings. And our swift, flapping a bit frantically, took up its life in an altogether new medium, the sky, airborne, beautifully flying, among its own. We could pick it out because it appeared slightly larger (beef-fed, after all) and because it flew with its tail spread out, the novice sacrificing speed for security.

It flew. We cheered and hugged.

The swifts and their cousins circled the neighborhood, tiny dots high in the sky. And Susanne and I watched for more than an hour, wondering why no symphonic crescendo accompanied this event, then knowing there *was* such an accompaniment—the silent burst of our own joy and awe and, yes, pride. We knew that an inconsequential birdling was now at home, that the others would follow, engaged in majestic flight, and that as soon as they got their tails together, they would become anonymous members of their race, taking swift-type risks at swiftian odds. Soon, with any luck at all, they would be in the upper Amazon basin.

Under federal law, raising foundling birds of certain species is not legal unless you have a license. We don't. But criminal as our act was, we now vicariously share the feeling of flight—a parental feeling if you will. And every summer for several years now we have been able to look into the clouds and say, "Hey, those are our birds!"

And each spring, we think again of the gift we received from those sooty little birds: a direct connection with one of those great and mysterious cycles of the planet.

*Currently living in New Mexico, **Jake Page** is the author of several books, including* Lords of the Air: The Smithsonian Book of Birds, Pastorale: A Natural History of Sorts, *and* Songs to Birds, *which includes this and other essays about bird life.*

Beach Meal, 1820

JAN ANNINO GODOWN

The beach is lit by the light of the moon
when she-bear pads along the shore

She stops
lifts wet snout into salted air
moves on

She repeats this testing until
the sniffing satisfies

She pads to a sandy place on strong feet
stops and digs

Sand and shell bits plume skyward
to snow back down on thick fur

She digs
she stops
shoves her mouth into a mound of white round balls

She tears and slurps the soft gift from the sea
a secret treasure chest

buried by a sea turtle mother
slashed by this land mother

She-bear shoulders through the palmetto thicket for home
frosted with smear of yolk
and glitter of sand

Jan Annino Godown *moved to Siesta Key near Sarasota as a child, and has been fascinated with Florida's natural wonders ever since. She now lives in Tallahassee with her husband and daughter, and is the author of two Florida guidebooks.*

Legend of the Swallow-tailed Kite

SUSAN CERULEAN

Unlike most places on earth, the state of Florida has lost its old, old stories. These stories—many of them about nature—disappeared when European conquistadors invaded the state between AD 1500 and 1800 and killed or drove out the native inhabitants. Embedded in these ancient tales was knowledge of how animals, including the human animal, could interact and cooperate with one another in a lasting fashion. In the spirit of those stories, author Susan Cerulean has created this story. It came to her through her observations of swallow-tailed kites over the last twenty years.

When the great mother gave birth to our planet, she could tell right away that it was a restless child, full of hot lava and great heat. She studied its spinning, saw how the water teetered up to the edges of the continents, sloshing. And she saw the continents, how they jostled one another, scrapping and pushing. How underneath the surface, the great tectonic plates, the uncertain bones of the earth, fought for position and space. She thought, "I need to give this globe-child of mine some structure here, or it may just fly apart!"

So the great mother gathered together the mammals, the birds, and all the other creatures, and gave to each a part in calming the planet whole. To the grazing animals, the bison and the elk and deer, she assigned the holding of the grass by their hooves; to the pelicans, the quieting of the sea waves.

It was to certain of the birds that she gave the job of tying together the northern and southern hemispheres: the phalarope and the least tern, the dowitcher and the spotted sandpiper, the vermilion flycatcher and the painted bunting. At that time, the swallow-tailed kite lived in the great open prairie lands of Brazil. The swallowtail had an exceptional ability to glide, although it looked more ordinary than it does today: its tail was no longer, nor more remarkable, than a hawk's.

The great mother took the swallowtail into her lap and knotted two enormous bobbins of invisible, sticky thread to the bird's outermost tail feathers. She instructed the kite to fly north over the high Andes, up the neck of Central America, and over Cuba, to North America.

The kite flew and flew on forceful wings, beating north, determined to fulfill its task—connecting the southern lands with those to the north. But as the kite began the last long leg of its journey, across the Gulf of Mexico, it encountered a powerful cold front, wave after wave of wind, and it had to fight and strain to stay on course to Florida. The pull of the thread on its tail was stronger than the earth mother had anticipated, but the mighty bird would not be stopped. By the time the bird dropped, exhausted, into the piney woods north of the Everglades, its outer tail feathers had been lengthened far beyond their original contour. But the bird's mission was fulfilled—the continents were securely stitched in place.

In this way, the kite became swallow-tailed. And every spring and fall, it still participates, together with the other migratory species, in a great weaving of the planet whole, a crisscrossing of

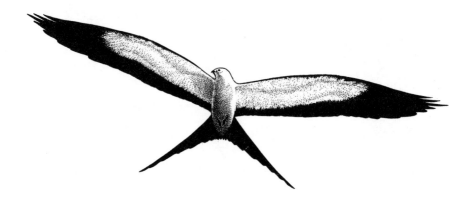

invisible threads, bringing just the necessary tension from South America to the Yukon. For this was what the great mother gave to the migratory birds to do, their part in providing us reassurance against the uncertain volcanoes, the great shifting tectonic plates, and the restless planet's spinning.

Susan Cerulean *has worked as a writer, wildlife biologist, and educator in Florida for the past twenty years. Her most recent publications are* The Book of the Everglades *and* Guide to the Great Florida Birding Trail: East Section. *Her nature memoir,* Tracking Desire: A Journey After Swallow-tailed Kites, *will be published by University of Georgia Press in February 2005.*

Waiting and Watching

ROBERT MURPHY

In his novel The Pond, *Robert Murphy depicts the adventures of a boy named Joey at his family's rural cabin near the Chickahominy Swamp in Virginia. Over the course of his visits, Joey befriends the cabin's elderly caretaker, named Ben, as well as a wary but loyal hunting dog named Charley. In this excerpt, Joey determines to seek out and kill a river otter that had nearly killed Charley in a fight just days before.*

He got up even earlier the next morning to be at the place at first light, and stayed there until the edge of darkness. No otter came past that day, or the next, or the day after. He began to wonder whether he had been wrong in his plan, but he stayed; he had an odd conviction that sooner or later he would see them. As the days followed one another, as he sat immobile in his hiding place or moved from the house to the place and back to the house again in the half-light when most of the wild creatures were returning to their dens or emerging from them, he saw more of their lives than he would have seen in a year of hunting. They weren't game in his mind now; he didn't think of shooting at them for fear of frightening or alerting the otters, and began to see them differently. Before, they had been targets, somewhat like animated but wary mechanical figures clothed in fur or feathers, to be outwitted, knocked over, and put into his game pocket; now they slowly turned into personalities with mannerisms and idiosyncrasies all their own.

He first noticed this in a solitary old raccoon which lived in a hollow in a big beech not far from his hiding place. It was a very large raccoon, and the first time he saw it it came ambling up the creek from its nocturnal wanderings early in the morning, pausing occasionally to turn over a stone in the creek bed. When it did this its paws, so much like little hands, seemed to have a life of their own; they felt all about while the old raccoon sat hunched, apparently not interested in them, and looked all about. As it came nearer it climbed out of the creek bed, walked a few steps, and turned back to the creek bed again. There was a light-colored stone near the falls; it went straight to that, felt all about beneath it, and left the creek bed again. When it came opposite Joey it stopped, turned its black highwayman's mask toward him, and froze. Although Joey hadn't moved and there was no wind, something told the old raccoon that an alien presence was there. It sat for a time, apparently weighing the mysterious intuition; several times it tensed as though to dash off, and relaxed again; finally it turned without haste, moved to the beech, climbed it, and disappeared into the hollow. Thereafter, when Joey was there, it paid little attention to the pine thicket. Oddly enough, it never investigated the thicket further but always avoided it; but no matter how it approached the beech it always made a detour to feel under the light-colored stone. During the day it occasionally came out of its hollow and sprawled over a limb to take a sunbath; it was company for a few of the long hours and fun to watch.

Several other raccoons wandered through the territory, but they all went through an elaborate series of maneuvers to investigate him; several deer passed, delicately moving and pretty, but only one of them was aware of him. That one startled him half out of his skin by approaching unheard and snorting loudly when it finally identified him. None of these animals stampeded off in fright after they had placed him but quietly withdrew; in some unfathomable way they seemed to know that he wasn't dangerous.

Others never knew he was there: a mink, dark and quick and lethal-looking as it worked the creek; two flying squirrels living near him that he often watched in the gloaming swooping down swift and shadowy between the darkening trees; a terrified rabbit and the bounding, sinuous weasel that pursued it; several hunting owls that went over him like ghosts in

the dusk. A possum almost walked across his legs one day and rolled over, grinning, to play dead when he moved. After a while it cautiously came back to life and died again when it saw he was still there; it went through this amusing performance several more times before it decided that he was harmless and went off, looking distrustfully back over its shoulder.

There were long periods when the woods were silent and empty. Between these empty and silent hours, however, he saw more than most people because he had more patience and more time, and in these hours he thought about the livelier ones.

The play of life about him, the clean and simple reasons for the actions of the creatures that he watched, their acuity and their moments of stress or calm or playfulness, brought him closer to them as time went on. He wondered about the enigmatic sixth sense that seemed to make them less assiduous in avoiding him than they had been before and made a start toward understanding it; unconsciously he was moving into a sympathy and concord with the animals around him, but he had a way to go yet. His feeling about the otters disturbed it, and if this feeling began to soften, he would remember the fight or Mr. Ben would mention that Charley had come looking for him and he would hate them again.

❧

Robert Murphy *lived in Virginia from the age of eight to eighteen. His family owned property on the edge of Chickahominy Swamp, a place he spent a great deal of time exploring. Although* The Pond *is fictional, it draws upon many of those boyhood experiences. Robert Murphy's other books include* The Peregrine Falcon *and* The Golden Eagle.

Bliss

RINA FERRARELLI

Here we are, inside, warm
and drying quickly,
feeling saved from the downpour
that thick and gray
blocks the view of the sound,
and there they are, the ducks,
below us, lit
by the large outdoor lamps,
white-speckled females
and sleek green-headed males
sitting and wiggling
in the pools among the rocks.
They splash water on their breasts,
wash under their raised wings,
dipping their beaks
first in the water, then
in their feathers,
step out, feet bright orange,
and stand still, glistening,
heads slightly tipped, eyes closed,
or while the rain keeps on falling,
pelting them, bury their beaks
in their feathers and seem to sleep.

Rina Ferrarelli's *poems and translations have been published in numerous journals, anthologies, and textbooks, and were collected in a book and in a chapbook of original poetry,* Home is a Foreign Country *(Eadmer Press, 1996) and* Dreamsearch *(malafemmina press, 1992), and in two books of translation. She has received an NEA grant, and the Italo Calvino Prize from the Columbia University Translation Center.*

Disturbing the Universe

BETSY HILBERT

Several species of sea turtles, all of them endangered, paddle in the waters off the South Atlantic coast. Laying a successful batch of eggs has become an enormous problem for these sea turtles because most of the wild, empty beaches they once visited have become the domain of our ever-growing human population. But if humans have the capacity to do harm, they also have the capacity to do good, a choice that Betsy Hilbert pursues in this essay.

Five thirty AM; the parking lot of Crandon Park is deserted. An empty plastic drinking cup crunches under the tires as we pull in. Nothing seems worth doing in the world this early. Ute and I climb groggily out of the car. Then the dawn blazes up out over the ocean, rose and gold across the sky. Everything has its compensations.

The beach is still in shadow under the brightening sky, and the dim figures of the morning cleanup crew make a clatter among the trash bins. The two of us are on a cleanup of a different kind this morning, amid the beachwracks and the crumpled potato chip bags.

"Seen anything?" my partner calls to one of the crew farther down the beach, who is slamming a trash can with particular vengeance.

"No, *Señora*," a voice drifts back, in the soft, mixed-ethnic accents of Miami. "No *tortugas* today."

Actually, we don't want the turtles themselves; it is the turtle eggs we're looking for, in their night-laid nests along this populous beach. Our job is to find and rescue the eggs of endangered loggerhead turtles, and to move them to a fenced area nearby maintained by the local Audubon Society, where the hatchlings can be safe from the picnickers and the beach-cleaning machines, and other dangers inherent on a public beach.

We begin our long walk south, where miles ahead the condominiums of Key Biscayne loom in the pale light. Pity the sea turtle who tries to climb their seawalls, or dig her nest in a carefully landscaped patch of St. Augustine grass. A series of grunts and swishes erupts behind us, as an early-morning beach jogger huffs past.

Ute's practiced strides take her up the beach almost faster than I can follow, distracted as I am by the pelican practicing hang-gliding in the morning air and the rippled sand in the tidal shallows. She stops suddenly, taking a soft breath, and I rush up to look. Leading upward from the high-water mark is a long, two-ridged scrape, balanced on either side by the zig-zag series of close, rounded alternating prints. Turtle crawl. Has she nested? Like all good predators, we sniff around a bit before deciding where to dig.

Just below the high dunes, in a circular patch about six feet across, the sand has been conspicuously flailed around. She has tried to discourage nest-robbers not by camouflage or hiding, but by leaving too much notice; the disturbed area is so big, and digging in the packed sand so difficult, that the attempt would discourage hunters with less sense of mission than we have. We could poke a sharp stick into the sand until it came up sticky with egg white, as is the traditional technique throughout the Caribbean, but that would damage eggs we are trying to protect. Nothing to do but start digging.

Beneath the turbulence of the dry top sand, the rough, damp subsurface scrapes against the skin of our hands. We run our fingers across the hard sand, hoping to find a soft spot. When no depression becomes apparent—this time it isn't going to be easy—we hand-dig trenches at intervals across the area. Sometimes it takes an hour or more of digging before the nest is found; sometimes there are no eggs at all.

In my third trench, about four inches down, there is a lump that doesn't feel like rock or shell. A smooth white surface appears, and another next to it slightly lower. The eggs look exactly like Ping-Pong balls, little white spheres, but the shell is soft and flexible. With infinite care, I lift the little balls out as Ute counts them, then place them in a plastic container, trying always to keep them in the same position they were laid. Turtle embryos bond to the shells, and turning the eggs as we rebury them might put the infants in the wrong position, with catastrophic results.

One hundred fourteen little worlds come out of their flask-shaped, smooth-sided nest. The eggs are spattered lightly with sand, and my probing fingers hit patches of sticky wetness among them, apparently some kind of lubricating fluid from the mother. The surprising softness of the shells makes sense to me as I dig deeper; hard shells might have cracked as the eggs dropped onto one another.

Carrying the egg container to the reburying place, I am glowing like the sunrise with self-satisfaction. Savior of sea turtles, that's me. Defender of the endangered. Momma turtle would be very pleased that her babies were receiving such good care.

Or would she? I look down at the eggs in their plastic box, and realize that she'd regard me as just another predator, if she regarded me at all. That turtle, if we ever met, would be much more concerned about my species' taste for turtle meat than about my professed interest in her offspring. What would I be to her except another kind of nuisance? Perhaps the Mother of Turtles might respond as the Pigeon in *Alice in Wonderland* does when Alice tries to explain that she's not a snake, but a little girl. "No, no! You're a serpent; and there's no use denying it. I suppose you'll be telling me next that you never tasted an egg!"

What was I to these eggs but just another nest-robber? Did I really know the impact of my actions, the extended chain of events I was setting in motion? With present scientific knowledge, no human alive could chart the course of that one loggerhead as she found her way across the seas. Where she bred and slept, where her food came from, are still mysteries. Not only are there too few scientists searching for the answers,

too little money for research, but ultimately there are "answers" we can probably never have. Our ways of knowing are species-locked, our understandings limited by human perceptual processes. I was a shadow on a dusky beach, groping in the dark for more than turtle eggs, digging, shoulder-deep, in holes not of my making.

Suppose we save these eggs, and the turtles that hatch return years later as hoped, to nest on this beach? This land will never be wild anymore; the skyscrapers that rise across Biscayne Bay bear megalithic testimony that the future of South Florida is written in concrete. The beach, if preserved, will continue public, and pressured, one of a small number of recreation areas for an ever-growing number of people. So there will never be a time when these animals can live out their lives without the intervention of people like Ute and me. Like so much else of nature now, the turtles of Crandon Park will be forever dependent on human action. Thanks to us, they are surviving; but thanks to us, they are also less than self-sufficient.

And why am I so convinced I'm actually doing good, anyway? Suppose more babies survive than can be supported by their environment, and next year there is a crash in their food supply, or that something we do, entirely unknowing, weakens the hatchlings so that their survival rate is actually lowered? Maybe we should just leave them alone. Maybe they would be better off taking their chances where their mothers first laid them, risking the raccoons and the beach parties.

None of us knows the final outcome of any action, the endless chain of ripples that we start with every movement. We walk in the world blindly, crashing into unidentified objects and tripping over rough edges. We human beings are too big for our spaces, too powerful for our understanding. What I do today will wash up somewhere far beyond my ability to know about it.

And yet, last year, five thousand new turtles were released from the Audubon compound, five thousand members of a threatened species, that would almost certainly not have been hatched otherwise. A friend who urged me to join the turtle project said that on a recent trip to Cape Sable in the Everglades he found at least fifteen nests on a short walk, every one of them dug up and destroyed by raccoons. Whatever chance these hundred fourteen embryos have, nestled inside their shells in the Styrofoam cradle, is what we give them.

In *The Encantadas,* his description of what are now called the Galápagos Islands, Herman Melville depicted the sea tortoises of "date-less, indefinite endurance," which the crew of the whaling ship takes aboard. Melville pointed out that those who see only the bright undersides of the tortoises might swear the animal has no dark side, while those who have never turned the tortoise over would swear it is entirely "one total inky blot." "The tortoise is both black and bright," Melville cautioned. So, too, my morning beach walk has two sides, one purposeful, the other full of doubt.

Whatever my ambivalences may be, the eggs are still in my hands. Ute and I reach the hatchery enclosure and unlock the chain-link fence. We dig another hole as close in size and shape to the original as we can imitate, and then rebury our babies, brushing our doubts back into the hole with the sand. As we mark the location of the new nest with a circle of wire fencing, I am reminded that in the world today there is no way, anymore, not to do something. Even if despite our best efforts there will never again be any loggerhead turtles, even if the numbers of the people concerned are few and our knowledge pitifully limited, even if we sometimes do unconscious harm in trying to do good, we no longer have the option of inaction. The universe is already disturbed, disturbed by more than my presence on an early-morning beach, with the sunlight glinting off the blue-tiled hotel swimming pools. While the choice is mine, I choose to walk.

Betsy Hilbert *was a professor of English at Miami-Dade Community College, where she focused on the study and teaching of nature literature.*

Appendixes

Ecology of the South Atlantic Coast and Piedmont

What Is an Ecoregion?

The *Stories from Where We Live* series celebrates the literature of North America's diverse ecoregions. Ecoregions are large geographic areas that share similar climate, soils, and plant and animal communities. Thinking ecoregionally helps us understand how neighboring cities and states are connected, and makes it easier to coordinate the use and protection of shared rivers, forests, watersheds, mountain ranges, and other natural areas. We believe that ecoregions also provide an illuminating way to organize and compare place-based literature.

While many institutions have mapped the world's ecoregions, no existing delineation of ecoregions (or similar unit, such as *provinces* or *bioregions*) proved perfectly suited to a literary series. We created our own set of ecoregions based largely on existing scientific designations, with an added consideration for regional differences in human culture.

THE

NORTHWEST

PACIFIC

COAST

BOREAL

GREAT

NORTH

ROCKY MOUNTAINS

CALIFORNIA

COAST

WESTERN

DESERTS

AND

PLATEAUS

HAWAIIAN

ISLANDS

ARCTIC

FOREST

AMERICAN

PRAIRIE

GREAT LAKES

NORTHEAST
WOODLANDS

NORTH

ATLANTIC

COAST

APPALACHIAN
HIGHLANDS

SOUTH
ATLANTIC
COAST
AND
PIEDMONT

SOUTHERN
HILL
COUNTRY

GULF COAST

Defining the South Atlantic Coast and Piedmont

If you were to draw a line from Baltimore to Atlanta to Miami, then follow the coastline back to Baltimore, you would demarcate almost perfectly the boundaries of the South Atlantic Coast and Piedmont. This vast ecoregion stretches across much of the southeastern United States, from the foothills of the Appalachians to the coastal waters of the Atlantic Ocean.

The western portion of the region is the Piedmont, rolling terrain named for the French word for "foot of the mountain." The eastern portion is the Atlantic coastal plain. The best way to get a sense for how these two regions fit together would be to travel the width of the South Atlantic Coast and Piedmont without modern day power. From the coastal waters of the Atlantic, you might nudge a sailing vessel into a broad river and sail smoothly upstream. For a while the land on either shore would be relatively flat and the river gentle. But farther up the river, your boat would encounter an impassable wall of rapids crashing down from upstream (or perhaps the wall of a dam). You'd have to pull ashore and continue the rest of your journey on horseback.

But this spot, where the land slopes steeply and the river churns with falls, would be an important landmark. It marks the "fall line"—the very place where the coastal plain gives way to the hills of the Piedmont. Continuing west, your horse would have little trouble negotiating the gentle rise and fall of the terrain. But eventually you'd notice the steep, rocky slope of mountains rising up before you. You'd be spared a laborious climb, though: those mountains, the Blue Ridge, mark the eastern edge of the Appalachians, and thus the end of your journey.

Understanding these three boundaries—the shore of the Atlantic Ocean, at sea level; the fall line, which occurs at about 500 feet; and the Appalachians, which rise from an elevation of about 1,500 feet—is key to understanding the eastern and western limits of the South Atlantic Coast and Piedmont ecoregion. Explaining its northern and southern borders is somewhat more complicated. Many scientists dub the area from the Canadian maritime provinces to Long Island the "north Atlantic," the area from Long Island to Cape Hatteras, North Carolina, the "mid-Atlantic," and the area from Cape Hatteras to southern Florida the "south Atlantic." In order to organize the Atlantic coastline into just two sections, we divided the mid-Atlantic portion in half at the Mason-Dixon line, recognizing the importance of culture in defining the northern and southern components of the Atlantic Coast.

The result is an ecoregion more than one thousand miles from north to south and in some places as much as 300 miles wide. Dozens of major rivers cross the region, tumbling from the higher elevations of the Piedmont down to the Atlantic. Beaches, salt marshes, and estuaries fringe the coast, and an uncommonly high number of narrow barrier islands lie parallel to the shore. Interior habitats range from forested hillsides in the Piedmont to swamps, bottomland forests, and pine flatlands on the coastal plain.

Large native groups, such as the Algonquins, Muscogee, and Waccama, thrived across this region for hundreds of years. Many of these groups were seminomadic, gathering shellfish at the coast in the spring, fruits and nuts in the Piedmont in the summer, and then moving into the mountains to hunt large game in the winter. By the time of European contact, many native groups had established large semi-permanent towns and farms. European contact was devastating for the region's Indians, however, and their populations plummeted due to introduced diseases, warfare, and forced relocation.

The first Europeans to reach the southeastern region were explorers who came to discover and gather the region's natural riches. By the 1600s, shiploads of Europeans began to establish colonies along the coast. Tobacco farming supported these colonies, as did the very lucrative trade in fur. In order to facilitate the movement of furs and other resources from the interior of the region out across the Atlantic, settlers sought to establish trading centers upriver. They sailed inland from coastal seaports, but, unable to overcome the inevitable rapids, stopped and built their trading centers right on the fall line. In later years, being so close to the rapids had a definite advantage: the fast-flowing water could be harnessed for power. Today, some of the region's largest cities, including Baltimore, Richmond, Columbia, and Augusta, still lie on the fall line—the outgrowth of those early, small trading centers.

Many people associate the South Atlantic Coast and Piedmont with mild climatic conditions, and they're not wrong. Conditions throughout the region are generally very favorable to living things. About forty inches of rain falls each year, spread out nicely across the months. In inland areas, winds average only about six to eight miles an hour, dramatically slower than the high winds that hit places such as the Midwest. Probably the greatest natural hazards of the region are the seasonal hurricanes that blast the coast, occasionally reaching into inland areas. But for most days of the year, the region offers a pleasant, hospitable environment.

Today the South Atlantic Coast and Piedmont boasts thriving universities, research centers, and industrial areas. Its cities have grown enormously in recent decades, and its citizenry becomes more vibrantly diverse each year. But in many ways, the region is still very much shaped by its natural resources. Tobacco and other forms of agriculture are still vital to the region's economy, as are the fisheries of the Chesapeake Bay and other coastal areas. Visitors and locals alike count on seeing the bursting blossoms of dogwoods and other flowering trees each spring, and flock to the shore each summer for a view of the great Atlantic.

Habitats

If you've spent time in the South Atlantic Coast and Piedmont region, you've undoubtedly observed shifts in the terrain—from the dunes and salt marshes that hug the coastline to inland rivers, fields, and forests. Each of these places is a *habitat*, a place that provides specific plants and animals with the food and environmental conditions they need to survive. Some animals are adapted to many different kinds of habitats; for example, a great blue heron can live in a salt marsh, lake, or river. Other animals are more selective: you won't find oysters venturing far from coastal estuaries. Protecting a diversity of habitats is essential, then, for preserving the diversity of life. Listed below are some of the dominant habitats you'll encounter in the South Atlantic Coast and Piedmont.

Beaches: Anyone who visits the same beach over and over again has undoubtedly noticed just how changeable beaches are. The tides rise and fall. Clouds gather and disperse. One day the shoreline is littered with debris from a recent storm; another day, the wind has swept it clean. Along the South Atlantic coast, beaches are especially dynamic, with relentless surf and strong, salty winds. Some days you may see no other living thing besides a wheeling gull or a few stalks of beach grass. Other days, you can witness some extraordinary wildlife sights. Along some parts of the coast, hordes of horseshoe crabs emerge from the sea each year to lay eggs, creating a crucial food source for bedraggled seabirds pausing on their lengthy migrations north and south. Endangered female sea turtles lug themselves ashore to visit the beaches of their birth and deposit their own clutch of eggs in pits in the sand. Elsewhere, flocks of migrating songbirds stop to rest in the stunted forests that lie behind the sandy dunes. Small herds of wild ponies roam the beaches of Assateague Island and Georgia's Cumberland Island.

In the South Atlantic region, sandy beaches line both the mainland coast and the seaward side of *barrier islands*—thin strips of land that lie parallel to the shore. In fact, the region boasts a great number of these barrier islands; if you've been to Assateague, the Outer Banks, or the Georgia sea islands, you've visited one of them. Barrier islands afford coastal communities critical protection from storms and high waves. Many of their beaches, as well as other southern Atlantic seashores, are protected seasonally or year-round to ensure safe shelter for beach-dependent creatures. (Examples: "On Assateague Island"; "Oystercatchers on the Moon"; "In the Dune Forest"; "Welcoming the Waves"; "Beach Meal, 1820"; "Disturbing the Universe.")

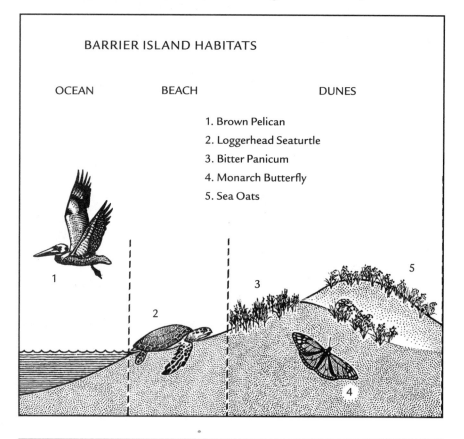

BARRIER ISLAND HABITATS

OCEAN   BEACH   DUNES

1. Brown Pelican
2. Loggerhead Seaturtle
3. Bitter Panicum
4. Monarch Butterfly
5. Sea Oats

Estuaries: If you floated downstream on any coastal river, you'd eventually reach the salty waters of the sea. But before your raft headed into the open ocean, it would pass through the transitional waters of an estuary. Estuaries form where freshwater and saltwater meet, and they're usually sheltered by islands or surrounding peninsulas. Loaded with nutrients from nearby salt marshes, estuaries offer a well-stocked pantry for hungry juvenile fish and shellfish. They also provide shelter for young fish, crabs, and other organisms in the form of offshore seagrass beds. Estuaries make such good nurseries, in fact, that most of the fish and shellfish we eat begin life in these habitats.

The largest estuary in America is the Chesapeake Bay, an exceptionally rich habitat located between the Maryland and Virginia mainland and the Delmarva Peninsula. Here scores of baby croakers, striped bass,

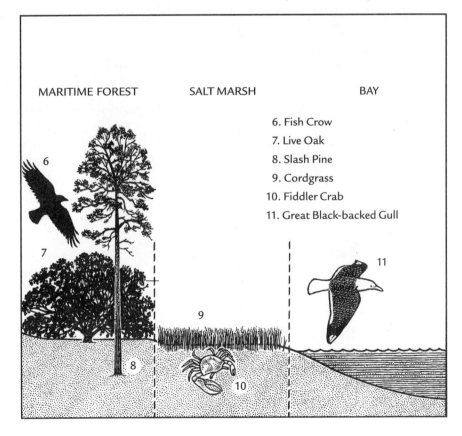

MARITIME FOREST   SALT MARSH   BAY

6. Fish Crow
7. Live Oak
8. Slash Pine
9. Cordgrass
10. Fiddler Crab
11. Great Black-backed Gull

sea robins, and other fish hatch in the sheltered waters. Blue crabs paddle about using specially shaped back legs, called swimmerettes. Herons ply for fish and frogs while oystercatchers pry apart partially-opened shells to get at the oyster or mussel inside. And oysters filter gallons of water each day, providing a natural cleaning system for the Bay. (Examples: "Chesapeake Homeplace"; "Oystering"; "Green Heron.")

Rivers and Streams: The rivers and streams that wend their way through the southern Piedmont and Atlantic coastal plain offer life support to land and water animals alike. Snakes, fish, frogs, birds, and turtles feast on aquatic insects, and in turn provide food for a number of larger animals. River otters careen down riverbanks and belly flop into the water where they snap up fish and frogs. Freshwater mussels and crayfish burrow in the river mud, a ready meal for trawling raccoons. Kingfishers plummet headfirst into the water to nab a passing fish. If the fish is too big for one swallow, they'll sit on a branch with the fish's tail sticking out of their beaks until their stomachs have digested the fish's head!

Because there are no glacial lakes in this region, many rivers have been dammed for recreation and power. The resulting declines in freshwater mussels, otters, and native fish and reptiles have inspired many people to work to protect the remaining southeastern rivers so they can continue to provide such vital habitat. (Examples: "Legacy"; "The Eco-Canoeist.")

Freshwater Wetlands: Every frog-lover and snake-seeker in the South Atlantic Coast and Piedmont has probably spent some time tromping through the soggy ground of one of the region's freshwater wetlands—marshes, swamps, and other moisture-rich areas. Found mostly in the low-lying coastal plain, freshwater wetlands also line the edges of many of the Piedmont's larger rivers, as well as small tributaries where beavers have built their dams. Wherever they exist, they support a mass of plant growth and supply food and shelter for insects, amphibians, reptiles, wading birds, and more. *Cypress bays,* named for their plentiful tall, swollen-trunked cypress trees, are among the distinctive wetlands of the South Atlantic Coast and Piedmont region. Rare *wet prairies* are another, abounding in sundews, sedges, meadow beauties, and other moisture-loving plants, not to mention great numbers of frogs and snakes. Georgia's Okefenokee Swamp, an extended mosaic of different wetland habitats, offers proof that wetlands are a reptile's dream habitat: it's home to an incredible fifteen thousand alligators! (Examples: "Into the Okefenokee"; "Paynes Prairie.")

Florida Scrub: In Florida, many people use the term "scrub" to refer to any area with sandy soils and stunted trees. The lack of nutrients in the sand, combined with frequent fires, keeps trees from attaining great heights. Sand pines tend to dominate these areas of scrub. But according to biologists, the truest kind of Florida scrub is very dry oak or pine-oak forest that grows along the state's central ridge line. Millions of years ago, when sea levels were higher, this ridge was a narrow sandy dune that provided the only barrier between the Gulf of Mexico to the west and the Atlantic Ocean to the east. Today it's home to Florida scrub jays sounding their raspy alarm calls from the trees, wild turkeys strutting along the forest floor in the company of white-tailed deer and black bears, and butterflies of every color bobbing among the flowers. (Examples: "Catch of the Day"; "Whooping Cranes.")

Pine Uplands: Hundreds of years ago, red-cockaded woodpeckers, gopher tortoises, eastern fox squirrels, and indigo snakes flourished in the more than seventy million acres of longleaf pine forest that covered the drier portion of the Atlantic coastal plain and a small part of the lower Piedmont. But today, fire suppression and timber cutting have reduced this forest to a series of patches totaling only about five percent of the original area. These remnants, where tall longleaf pines grow above a carpet of wire grass, are essential to the survival of many threatened species. Red-cockaded woodpeckers carve their nest holes in the trunks of old pine trees whose centers have been softened by rot. Wild turkeys and bobwhite quails feast on a profusion of longleaf pine seeds. Gopher tortoises excavate their burrows in the dry, sandy soils. These burrows, in turn, provide critical shelter for indigo snakes, diamondback rattlesnakes, gopher frogs, Florida mice, and hundreds of other creatures, especially when fires blaze through the understory. The fires are ultimately life-giving for the forest, clearing out other vegetation that might compete with the old longleaf pines, and allowing new pine seedlings to take root in the blackened soil. (Examples: "Longleaf"; "Gopher Tortoise Lament.")

Southern Piedmont Forests: Much like longleaf pine forests, the southern Piedmont forests have changed a lot since the days before European settlement. Once dominated by towering mature oaks and hickories, they now consist mostly of loblolly and shortleaf pines interspersed with hardwoods such as southern red oak, sweet gum, tulip poplar, and pignut hickory. If you hike through these forests, you'll still have a chance to encounter a great variety of wild creatures. Carolina chickadees hop from branch to branch. Gray squirrels and chipmunks scurry about. Virginia opossums amble across the ground. Great horned owls swoop down from the canopy and pounce upon a passing mouse or shrew. (Examples: "The Fort"; "Tiger of the Air.")

Suburbs and Cities: People are plentiful in the South Atlantic Coast and Piedmont region, and they've altered the landscape by building cities and suburbs, by clearing forests for farms, and through other activities. Human development doesn't have to translate into an absence of wildness, though. In many cities and suburbs, wild creatures persist in vacant lots, city trees, parks, and more. For example, you might notice woodpeckers drilling into a tree in your school yard or raccoons feasting from overflowing garbage cans. Amazingly enough, some of the largest trees left in the eastern United States grow in residential suburbs and city parks. In the best of circumstances, people in developed areas have made special efforts to accommodate their furred and feathered neighbors. The creation of Rock Creek Park in Washington, D.C., has given refuge to barred owls and red-shouldered hawks. The Duke Forest in Durham, North Carolina, protects one of the last fragments of southern Piedmont oak-hickory forest and is home to wood pewees, wild turkeys, and whip-poor-wills. And in Atlanta and other cities, residents are taking part in programs to make their backyards havens for songbirds, butterflies, and other species. (Examples: "Jack's Kite"; "Back of the Pack"; "Bounty"; "Swifts at Evening.")

Animals and Plants

Among the many animals and plants found in the South Atlantic Coast and Piedmont ecoregion are the following species that appear in the literature of this anthology.

Birds: If you spend time in the South Atlantic Coast and Piedmont region, you're sure to be impressed by the number and variety of birds. *Ducklike birds* of the region include grebes, mute swans and other swans, Canada geese, coots, wood ducks, mallards, teals, and mergansers. At the shore, you'll spy *seabirds,* also known as *aerialists,* such as pelicans and gulls. Great blue herons, green herons, night herons, egrets, storks, sandhill cranes, whooping cranes, and ibises are all *long-legged wading birds* that favor wetland habitats. *Smaller wading birds* include American oystercatchers, plovers, sanderlings, and spotted sandpipers. Among the region's *fowl-like birds* are bobwhites and other quails. Its *birds of prey* include swallow-tailed kites, harrier hawks, eagles, ospreys, barred owls, great horned owls (also known as hoot owls), and burrowing owls. *Nonperching land birds* include whip-poor-wills, nighthawks (sometimes called bullbats), kingfishers, pileated woodpeckers, red-cockaded woodpeckers, and chimney swifts. Many *perching birds* live in this region, including purple martins, barn swallows, crows, catbirds, red-winged blackbirds, starlings, warblers, and cardinals.

Wood Duck

Great Blue Heron

Kingfisher

Mammals: Dolphins and porpoises are among the marine mammals that swim along the Atlantic coast. Land mammals of the coast and Piedmont include Florida mice, rats, chipmunks, flying squirrels and other squirrels, cottontails and other rabbits, armadillos, opossums, raccoons, round-tailed muskrats, mink, weasels, otters, bats, foxes, Florida panthers, black bears, deer, and wild horses.

Flying Squirrel

Otter

Marine Invertebrates: Marine invertebrates are sea creatures that don't have a backbone. They're subdivided into different groups. For example, jellyfish are *jellylike animals.* Oysters and squid are *mollusks.* And shrimp and crabs, such as blue crabs, are *crustaceans.* Crabbers often refer to female crabs as sooks and male crabs as Jimmies.

Blue Crab

Freshwater and Terrestrial Invertebrates: Among the region's many terrestrial invertebrates (land animals without a backbone) are earthworms and a group of organisms known as *arachnids,* which includes giant ticks and other ticks, wolf spiders and other spiders, and chiggers. *Insects* make up a huge subgroup of terrestrial invertebrates that includes such creatures as dragonflies, doodlebugs (also known as ant lions), praying mantises, katydids, crickets, scarab beetles and other beetles, mealworms (the larval form of certain beetles), lightning bugs, flies, mosquitoes, pine bugs, ants, wasps, bumblebees, and moths. Freshwater snails are some of the region's many freshwater invertebrates.

Field Cricket

Reptiles and Amphibians: The South Atlantic Coast and Piedmont is paradise for reptiles and amphibians. *Reptiles* have claws on their feet (if they have feet), and their skin is dry and scaly. This group includes painted turtles, stinkpot turtles, snapping turtles, box turtles, gopher tortoises, loggerhead sea turtles and other sea turtles, alligators, skinks, anoles, lizards, diamondback rattlesnakes, cotton-mouth moccasins, hognose snakes, Eastern indigo snakes, and Florida pine snakes. *Amphibians* are clawless with moist skin, lay their eggs in the water, and go through a change called metamorphosis when they are young. The group includes pig frogs, tree frogs, gopher frogs, bullfrogs, and toads.

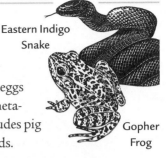

Eastern Indigo Snake

Gopher Frog

Striped Mullet

Fish: Among the many *freshwater fish* of the region are largemouth bass and other bass, trout, and bowfins. Striped bass, bluefish, croaker, striped mullet, spot, and red snapper are among the myriad *saltwater fish* that frequent coastal areas.

Plants: Mosses and ferns are two types of spore plants of the South Atlantic Coast and Piedmont. Among the *needleleaf trees* of the region are cedars, cypresses, and longleaf pines and other pines. *Large, broadleaf trees* include Australian pines, live oaks and other oaks, elms, sassafras, magnolias, tulip trees, maples, red mulberries, ailanthus, ficus, palms, cabbage palmettos and saw palmettos, hickories, weeping willows and other willows, sweet gum, Chinese chestnuts, cherry trees, pear trees, orange trees, crepe myrtles, ginkgos, banyans, and avocado trees. *Small broadleaf trees and shrubs* include pawpaw, bayberry, Brazilian pepper, Key lime, buttonbush, azalea, gardenia (Cape Jasmine), frangipani, night-blooming jasmine, ixora, Surinam cherry, wineberry, oleander, camellia, quince, crotons, holly, boxwood, and scrub palmetto. Broadly speaking, the following are *wildflowers* of the region: rabbit tobacco (also known as sweet everlasting), dog fennel, cattail, poison ivy, St. Augustine grass, wire grass, zoysia, hibiscus, honeysuckle, wisteria, bougainvillea, alamanda, orchids, roses, kudzu, pokeweed, strawberries, sedges, sawgrass,

Longleaf Pine

Wisteria

bulrush, water lilies and other lilies, and purple liatris. A substantial number of the plants listed above are not native to the region, but have been transplanted from other warm habitats for ornamental and other purposes.

Others: Oyster mushrooms and other mushrooms are in a special group of organisms called *fungi.* Seaweed is part of a group of organisms known as *algae.* Neither fungi nor algae are now considered part of the plant family.

Stories by State

Florida

1. "Summer of Being Ten" (West Palm Beach)
2. "Welcoming the Waves" (Fort Lauderdale)
3. "Coming of Age in the Tropics" (West Palm Beach)
4. "Ponte Vedra Beach" (Ponte Vedra Beach)
5. "Paynes Prairie" (near Gainesville)
6. "Catch of the Day" (Lake County)
7. "Freeze" (north-central Florida)
8. "The Eco-Canoeist" (Orlando)
9. "Alligators" (St. Johns River)
10. "Whooping Cranes" (now Ocala National Forest)
11. "Gopher Tortoise Lament" (Putnam and Clay County sandhills)
12. "Beach Meal, 1820" (Cape Canaveral)
13. "Legend of the Swallow-tailed Kite" (southcentral Florida)
14. "Disturbing the Universe" (Miami)

Georgia

15. "Into the Okefenokee" (Okefenokee Swamp)
16. "The Fort" (Powder Springs)
17. "Longleaf" (Baxley)
18. "Lessons of the Road: Crossing the Florida-Georgia State Line" (Folkston)
19. "A February Walk in Georgia" (Athens)

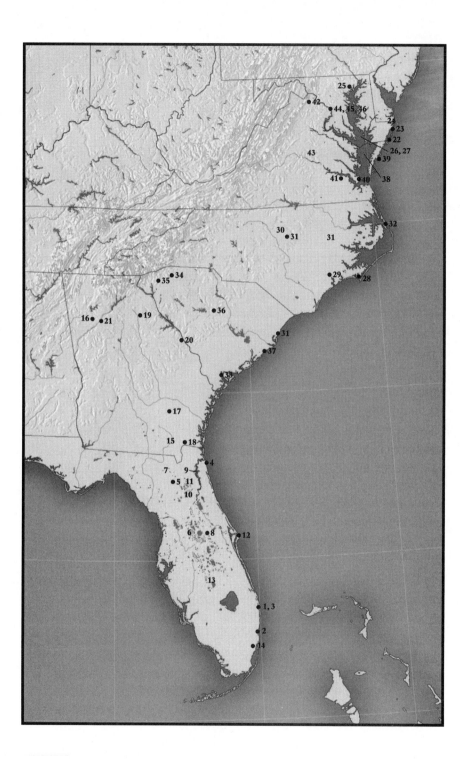

Washington, D.C.

Parks and Preserves

Listed below are just a few of the many places where you can go to experience the wilder side of the South Atlantic Coast and Piedmont ecoregion. Bear in mind that some of these states straddle more than one ecoregion, so we have included only those natural areas that lie in the coastal plain or Piedmont portions of the state. Also, please note that the phone numbers provided are sometimes for the park's headquarters, but often are for a managing agency or organization. In any case, the people at these numbers can provide you with details about the area and directions for how to get there.

Florida

Arthur R. Marshall Loxahatchee National Wildlife Refuge (Boynton Beach) 561-734-8303

Biscayne National Park (Homestead) 305-230-7275

Guana River State Park and Guana River Wildlife Management Area (South Ponte Vedra Beach) 904-825-5071

Jonathan Dickinson State Park (Hobe Sound) 772-546-2771

Lake Wales Ridge State Forest (Frostproof) 863-635-7801

Little Talbot Island State Park (Jacksonville) 904-251-2320

Merritt Island National Wildlife Refuge and Canaveral National Seashore (Titusville) 321-861-0667

Mike Roess Gold Head Branch State Park (Keystone Heights) 352-473-4701

Ocala National Forest (Silver Springs) 352-625-2520

Osceola National Forest (Lake City) 386-752-2577

Paynes Prairie (Micanopy) 352-466-4100

Pelican Island National Wildlife Refuge (Sebastian) 772-562-3909

Tosohatchee State Reserve (Christmas) 407-568-5893
Wekiwa Springs State Park (Apopka) 407-884-2008

Georgia

Banks Lake National Wildlife Refuge (Lakeland) 912-496-7366
Blackbeard Island National Wildlife Refuge 912-652-4415
Callaway Gardens (Pine Mountain) 706-663-2281
Cumberland Island National Seashore 912-882-4336
Little St. Simons Island Resort 912-638-7472
Oconee National Forest (Eatonton) 770-297-3000
Okefenokee National Wildlife Refuge (Folkston) 912-496-7836
Panola Mountain State Conservation Park (Stockbridge)
    770-389-7801
Piedmont National Wildlife Refuge (Round Oak) 478-986-5441
Sapelo Island National Estuarine Research Reserve 912-437-3224
Savannah National Wildlife Refuge (Savannah) 912-652-4415
Wassaw National Wildlife Refuge (Wassaw Island) 912-652-4415

Maryland

Assateague Island National Seashore (Berlin) 410-641-1441
Blackwater National Wildlife Refuge (Cambridge) 410-228-2677
Calvert Cliffs State Park (Lusby) 301-743-7613
Cedarville State Forest (Waldorf) 301-888-1410
Eastern Neck National Wildlife Refuge (Rock Hall) 410-639-7056
Gunpowder Falls State Park (Kingsville) 410-592-2897
Janes Island State Park (Crisfield) 410-968-1565
Sandy Point State Park (Annapolis) 410-974-2149
Soldiers Delight Natural Environment Area (Owings Mills)
    410-922-3044

North Carolina

Bladen Lakes Educational State Forest (Elizabethtown) 910-588-4964
Cape Hatteras National Seashore (Cape Hatteras) 252-473-2111
Cape Lookout National Seashore (Harkers Island) 252-728-2250
Cliffs of the Neuse State Park (Seven Springs) 919-778-6234

Duke Forest (Durham) 919-613-8013

Great Dismal Swamp National Wildlife Refuge (see Virginia)
757-986-3705

Jordan Lake State Recreation Area (Apex) 919-362-0586

Mackay Island National Wildlife Refuge (Knotts Island) 252-429-3100

Nags Head Woods Ecological Preserve (Kill Devil Hills) 252-441-2525

Pea Island National Wildlife Refuge (Rodanthe) 252-473-1131

Pocosin Lakes National Wildlife Refuge (Creswell) 252-796-3004

Uwharrie National Forest (Troy) 910-576-6391

South Carolina

Ace Basin National Wildlife Refuge (Hollywood) 843-889-3084

Cape Romain National Wildlife Refuge (Awendaw) 843-928-3368

Carolina Sandhills National Wildlife Refuge (McBee) 843-335-8401

Congaree Swamp National Monument (Gadsden) 803-776-4396

Flat Creek Heritage Preserve and Forty Acre Rock (Lancaster County)
803-734-3893

Francis Beidler Forest (Harleyville) 843-462-2150

Francis Marion National Forest (McClellanville and Cordeville)
843-887-3257 and 843-336-3248

Hitchcock Woods Natural Area (Aiken) 803-642-0528

Huntington Beach State Park (Murrells Inlet) 843-237-4440

Lewis Ocean Bay Heritage Preserve (Conway) 843-546-3226

Santee National Wildlife Refuge (Summerton) 803-478-2217

Tom Yawkey Wildlife Center (Georgetown) 843-546-6814

Woods Bay State Park (Olanta) 843-659-4445

Virginia

Back Bay National Wildlife Refuge (Virginia Beach) 757-721-2412

Caledon Natural Area (Fredericksburg) 540-663-3861

Chincoteague National Wildlife Refuge (Assateague Island)
757-336-6122

Cumberland State Forest (Farmville) 804-492-4121

Great Dismal Swamp National Wildlife Refuge (Suffolk)
757-986-3705

Huntley Meadows Park (Alexandria) 703-768-2525
James River Park (Richmond) 434-933-4355
Occoneechee State Park (Clarksville) 434-374-2210
Kiptopeke State Park (Cape Charles) 757-331-2267
Lake Anna State Park (Mineral) 540-854-5503
Mason Neck National Wildlife Refuge (Lorton) 703-490-4979
Scotts Run Nature Preserve (McLean) 703-759-9018
Virginia Coast Reserve (Exmore) 757-442-3049

Washington, D.C.

Chesapeake and Ohio National Historic Park (Cumberland,
    Maryland, to D.C.) 301-739-4200
Rock Creek Park 202-895-6070

Recommended Reading

Alden, Peter, Brian Cassie, et al. *National Audubon Society Field Guide to the Mid-Atlantic States.* New York: Alfred A. Knopf, 1999.

Alden, Peter, Rick Cech, Gil Nelson, et al. *National Audubon Society Field Guide to Florida.* New York: Alfred A. Knopf, 1998.

Alden, Peter, Gil Nelson, et al. *National Audubon Society Field Guide to the Southeastern States.* New York: Alfred A. Knopf, 1999.

Amos, William, and Stephen H. Amos. *Atlantic and Gulf Coasts.* (Audubon Society Nature Guides). New York: Alfred A. Knopf, 1985.

Godfrey, Michael A. *A Sierra Club Naturalist's Guide to the Piedmont.* San Francisco: Sierra Club Books, 1980.

Gosner, Kenneth L., and Roger Tory Peterson. *A Field Guide to the Atlantic Seashore.* Boston: Houghton Mifflin, 1999.

Hay, John, and Peter Farb. *The Atlantic Shore: Human and Natural History from Long Island to Labrador.* New York: Harper & Row, 1966.

Kochanoff, Peggy. *Beachcombing the Atlantic Coast.* Missoula, Mont.: Mountain Press, 1997.

Lippson, Alice James. *Life in the Chesapeake.* Baltimore: Johns Hopkins University Press, 1997.

Miller, Arthur P. Jr., and Marjorie L. Miller. *Park Ranger Guide to Seashores.* Harrisburg: Stackpole Books, 1992.

Special Thanks

Editing the *Stories from Where We Live* anthologies is part treasure hunt and part casting call.

The treasure hunt takes the form of searches for existing material suitable for each volume—combing through magazines, historical materials, novels, poetry collections, and even other anthologies to try to locate quality material that can be reprinted in these pages. Occasionally my search benefits from the assistance of readers with sharp eyes and keen memories. In this case, I owe special thanks to my mother, Lloyd St. Antoine, for sending me several worthy resources from the region, and to my mother-in-law, Cynthia Cone, both for remembering her fondness of Robert Murphy's *The Pond* and for still having it on her shelves.

The casting call part of the editing process involves sending out notices to writers and inviting them to make submissions to a particular region's anthology. The ensuing onslaught of material from every corner of the region is a pleasant bombardment indeed, and provides me with the bulk of each anthology's selections. For this volume, I also tried a variation on the casting call, pinpointing several friends with close ties to the region and inviting them to try their hand at a story or essay. The results were marvelous, and I want to personally thank the three of you (you know who you are) for taking the risks you did. I hope you agree that it was worth the effort.

I also want to thank Betsy Teter of the Hub City Writers Group for sending me material from her organization. As always, a great big hug and thanks to Priscilla Howell, Robin Kelsey, Jen Kretser, and Jen Lindstrom for reading the first draft of this anthology and commenting on the selections. And, finally, enormous thanks to Al Tate, ecologist at Fernbank Science Center in Atlanta, and Richard Osorio, coordinator for the Georgia Project for Excellence in Environmental Education. Their critical response to the Invitation and Appendixes was invaluable, and any remaining errors are my own.

Contributor Acknowledgments

Day Alexander, "Potomac and the Gray Swan." Copyright © 2004 by Day Alexander. Printed with permission from the author.

Kimberly Greene Angle, "The Fort." Copyright © 2004 by Kimberly Greene Angle. Printed with permission from the author.

Katherine S. Balch, "Anna's Tenth Summer," *Cricket* 25, no. 11 (July 1998): 4–8. Copyright © 1998 by Katherine S. Balch. Reprinted with permission from the author.

William Bartram, "Alligators," excerpted from "Travels" in *Travels and Other Writings* (New York: Library of America, 1996), 117–18.

P. G. Brake, "Hampton Wetlands." Copyright © 2004 by P. G. Brake. Printed with permission from the author.

Archie Carr, "Paynes Prairie," excerpted from "The Bird and the Behemoth" in *A Naturalist in Florida: A Celebration of Eden,* ed. Marjorie Harris Carr (New Haven: Yale University Press, 1994), 14–16. Copyright © 1964 by Archie Carr. Reprinted with permission from the Estate of Archie Carr.

Susan Cerulean, "Legend of the Swallow-tailed Kite." Copyright © 2004 by Susan Cerulean. Printed with permission from the author.

Mary Ann Coleman, "A February Walk in Georgia," *Cricket* 25, no. 6 (February 1998). Copyright © 1998 by Mary Ann Coleman. Reprinted with permission from the author.

McCabe Coolidge, "A Peek." Copyright © 2004 by McCabe Coolidge. Printed with permission from the author.

C. W. Dingman, "Into the Okefenokee." Copyright © 2004 by C. W. Dingman. Printed with permission from the author.

Rina Ferrarelli, "Bliss," *MacGuffin* 18, no. 1 (2001). Copyright © 2001 by Rina Ferrarelli. Reprinted with permission from the author.

Gretchen Fletcher, "Coming of Age in the Tropics," *Chattahoochee Review* 21, no. 3 (Spring 2001): 78–79. Copyright © 2001 by Gretchen Fletcher. Reprinted with permission from the author. "Summer of Being Ten,"

A Summer's Reading, no. 6 (2002): 81. Copyright © 2002 by Gretchen Fletcher. Reprinted with permission from the author.

Martin Galvin, "Heron Bay," *Commonweal* 126 (September 28, 1979): 534. Copyright © 1979 by Martin Galvin. Reprinted with permission from the author.

Jan Annino Godown, "Beach Meal, 1820." Copyright © 2004 by Jan Annino Godown. Printed with permission from the author.

Susan Gray Gose, "Back of the Pack." Copyright © 2004 by Susan Gray Gose. Printed with permission from the author.

Jeffrey Harrison, "Swifts at Evening," in *Signs of Arrival* (Providence: Copper Beech Press, 1996), 60. Copyright © 1996 by Jeffrey Harrison. Reprinted with permission from Copper Beech Press.

Gary Henderson, "Jack's Kite," in *Hub City Anthology,* ed. John Lane and Betsy Teter (Spartanburg: Holocene Publishing, 1996), 31–36. Copyright © 1996 by Gary Henderson. Reprinted with permission from the author.

Betsy Hilbert, "Disturbing the Universe," in *Being in the World: An Environmental Reader for Writers,* ed. Scott H. Slovic and Terrell F. Dixon (New York: Macmillan Publishing, 1994), 229–33. Previously published in *Orion Magazine* 6, no. 3 (Summer 1987): 63–65. Copyright © 1987 by The Myrin Institute. Reprinted with permission from *Orion Magazine.*

Paul Jahnige, "Bounty." Copyright © 2004 by Paul Jahnige. Printed with permission from the author.

Mélina Mangal, "Welcoming the Waves." Copyright © 2004 by Mélina Mangal. Printed with permission from the author.

Mary E. Mebane, Excerpt from *Mary* (New York: Penguin Putnam, 1981), 18–22. Copyright © 1981 by Mary Elizabeth Mebane. Reprinted with permission from Viking Penguin, a division of Penguin Putnam, Inc.

Ann E. Michael, "Green Heron," *White Pelican Review* 2, no. 2 (Fall 2000): 26. Copyright © 2000 by Ann E. Michael. Reprinted with permission from the author.

Felicia Mitchell, "My Country Garden," *Potato Eyes* 11 & 12 (Fall/Winter/Spring 1995–96): 35. Copyright © 1995 by Felicia Mitchell. Reprinted with permission from the author.

Sy Montgomery, "The Eco-Canoeist," excerpted from "The Eco-Canoeist," *Orion Afield* 4, no. 2 (Spring 2000): 32–33. Copyright © 2000 by Sy Montgomery. Reprinted with permission from the author.

Lenard D. Moore, "A Haiku and Two Tanka," in *Spirit and Flame: An Anthology of Contemporary African American Poetry,* ed. Keith Gilyard (Syracuse

About the Editor

Sara St. Antoine grew up in Ann Arbor, Michigan. She holds a bachelor's degree in English from Williams College and a master's degree in environmental studies from the Yale School of Forestry and Environmental Studies. Currently living in Cambridge, Massachusetts, she enjoys walking along the Charles River and seeing black-crowned night herons hunkered in the trees.

About the Illustrators

Paul Mirocha is a designer and illustrator of books about nature for children and adults. His first book, *Gathering the Desert*, by Gary Paul Nabhan, won the 1985 John Burroughs Medal for natural history. He lives in Tucson, Arizona, with his daughters, Anna and Claire.

Trudy Nicholson is an illustrator of nature with a background in medical and scientific illustration. She received her B.S. in fine arts at Columbia University and has worked as a natural-science illustrator in a variety of scientific fields for many years. She lives in Cabin John, Maryland.

Milkweed Editions

Founded in 1979, Milkweed Editions is one of the largest independent, nonprofit literary publishers in the United States. Milkweed publishes with the intention of making a humane impact on society, in the belief that great writing can transform the human heart and spirit. Within this mission, Milkweed publishes in four areas: fiction, nonfiction, poetry, and children's literature for middle-grade readers.

Join Us

Milkweed depends on the generosity of foundations and individuals like you, in addition to the sales of its books. In an increasingly consolidated and bottom-line-driven publishing world, your support allows us to select and publish books on the basis of their literary quality and the depth of their message. Please visit our Web site (www.milkweed.org) or contact us at (800) 520-6455 to learn more about our donor program.

Interior design by Wendy Holdman.
Typeset in 12/16 point Legacy Book
by Stanton Publication Services, Inc.
Printed on acid-free 55# Fraser Trade Book paper
by Friesen Corporation.